PENGUIN BUSINESS
EMOTIONAL INCLUSION®

Mollie Rogers Jean De Dieu is the General Manager of French fashion and accessory company, Longchamp, in Singapore and Malaysia, a keynote speaker, and Founder of Emotional Inclusion®, a non-profit organization where she exercises passionate advocacy for humanizing the workforce.

A seasoned veteran of the people industry, Mollie has listened to and witnessed countless stories of individuals struggling to navigate work while facing the 'perfect storm'. Over her two-decade-long career, Mollie has grappled with the reality of the subject matter and the urgent need to advocate a safe platform where emotions can be heard, recognized, and dealt with. Today, Mollie champions a new paradigm of corporate leadership with Emotional Inclusion® that requires companies to recognize and care for the humanity of the individuals they lead by investing in tailored, emotionally inclusive medical, mental health pillars.

Mollie's work—through her organization and its programs—draws on the latest research in positive and behavioural psychology, leadership development, and organizational change. Through her Emotional Inclusion® podcast (available on iTunes/Spotify), Mollie hosts renowned global leaders who are advocates for emotionally inclusive workplaces. She ultimately aims to shatter the business landscape's archaic status quo by leading the way to a wholesome, new mindset in the workforce.

A self-proclaimed citizen of the world, Mollie grew up between Africa, France, the United States, and has made Asia her home for the past seventeen years. She spent nine years in Hong Kong and eight years in Singapore, where she currently resides with her family.

Emotional Inclusion®
A Humanizing Revolution
at Work

Mollie Rogers Jean De Dieu

BUSINESS
An imprint of Penguin Random House

PENGUIN BUSINESS

USA | Canada | UK | Ireland | Australia
New Zealand | India | South Africa | China | Southeast Asia

Penguin Business is part of the Penguin Random House group of companies
whose addresses can be found at global.penguinrandomhouse.com

Published by Penguin Random House SEA Pvt. Ltd
9, Changi South Street 3, Level 08-01,
Singapore 486361

First published in Penguin Business by Penguin Random House SEA 2023
Copyright © Mollie Rogers Jean De Dieu 2023

ISBN 9789815058185

Typeset in Garamond by MAP Systems, Bengaluru, India

www.penguin.sg

To Charles, Mia, and Louis—my three children, the first of them in heaven—for whom my love transcends all space and time

Contents

Foreword											ix

Emotional Inclusion® Defined								1

A New Organizational Platform								18

The Stigma										42

What Global Leaders Have to Say								59

The Humanization of Work								79

Inclusion is an Action									132

A New, Emotionally-Inclusive Era							147

Final Thoughts										163

Acknowledgements									173

Foreword

It gives me great pleasure to write a foreword to Mollie Rogers Jean De Dieu's wise, honest, timely book. As a scholar of management, I was overjoyed to meet a business leader who brings practical wisdom to her role as general manager (at Longchamp Singapore and Malaysia), while also doing the hard work of sharing this wisdom with a wider audience. To put my thoughts into context, I teach a course at Harvard Business School on how to become an effective general manager. General managers occupy a senior role that necessarily confronts difficult decisions while being responsible for inspiring and enabling others to work together to achieve challenging goals. It is in this capacity that I was fortunate to discover Mollie and her ideas, and now I am privileged to set the stage for you to do so as well.

If all general managers had the insight and compassion that Mollie brings both to her leadership role at Longchamp and to her advocacy in her book and in her popular podcast, we would live in a palpably better world. In the meantime, Mollie is on a personal quest to help us get there. Fortunately, what she describes and advocates in this wonderful book is remarkably aligned with the ideas and skills I seek to develop in the aspiring managers in my MBA classroom. These skills are both invaluable and rare. But what truly matters is that they *can* be learned.

I teach my students that the most effective general managers are those who are fully aware of the complexity of the role. Consider what it means to be responsible for ensuring coordinated action in pursuit of performance that serves the needs of customers, employees, and investors alike! In a dynamic and interconnected world, these challenges, which are both intellectual and emotional, are formidable. Those who fail to reflect deeply on them will invariably come up short. Reflection is a first step, but it must be followed by an iterative cycle of action, feedback, and more reflection.

My research has long emphasized the centrality of *learning*—individual, team, and organizational—as a cornerstone to navigating the challenges we face in an uncertain world. These days I see this as a valid but incomplete perspective. Quite simply, it downplays the role of emotions. Perhaps because I started my career as an engineer, I was convinced that analysis and problem solving mattered more than 'feelings' (which Mollie is quick to point out are not synonymous with emotions). Then I became a scholar of organizational behaviour and management, and my research had a mind of its own, allowing me to discover the importance of emotions. In a fast-moving world—where we are dependent on ingenuity and collaboration to get challenging and novel work done—we are most productive when we feel good about who we are, what we bring, and how we work with others. Fulfilment, happiness, and good performance come from meaningful engagement with colleagues we respect and trust. And this engagement, I have found, happens best in a psychologically safe environment where people believe that they can speak up candidly about ideas, questions, concerns, and mistakes. But despite the now extensive body of research on this concept, we still have work to do in translating these findings into action. This book can help.

Mollie puts the spotlight on Emotional inclusion as a crucial aspect of making work more humane and more effective. Although recognition of the importance of Emotional intelligence has increased in recent years, what many do not fully appreciate is that Emotional intelligence and inclusion start with confronting our own shortcomings. This can be painful, especially for high achievers. Yet, as you shall soon see—and as the quote that opens Mollie's book emphasizes—it must be endured if we are to reach a better place. Workplaces with greater psychological safety and Emotional inclusion will make it possible for everyone to contribute and thrive. If you are one of the many people who remain skeptical that such a work environment is possible, read on. This book will show you that it is—through Mollie's own voice, informed by her years of experience in the people-intensive industry context of retail, and amplified by the voices of several other remarkable business leaders who span industries and countries. It is their stories that come alive in the pages of this book and give me hope that we may be heading in the right direction.

Mollie argues that managers have a moral duty to act in ways that appreciate what it means to be human at work. I agree. Every one of us can impact one another's life, positively or negatively, at pivotal moments. As she explains, we do this through kindness, but also, and perhaps most importantly, we do this by living our values. Our actions constitute the strongest message of all. But it is not always easy to live your values. One of my most treasured mentors, Harvard Professor Chris Argyris, wrote of the gap between our espoused and lived values. As Chris showed, this gap does not arise due to hypocrisy or insincere commitment to stated values. Rather, it arises due to powerful cognitive and Emotional forces that lead us to privilege control and face-saving over learning and genuine relationships with others. But, through self-awareness and curiosity, the gap can be closed with practice.

This book is no mere philosophical exercise; Mollie speaks directly to the practical challenges of management, showing how to practice the Emotional labour of being a manager in a way that will work for you and for your teams. These skills may not be effortless, but there is much in the pages ahead to help you develop and practice them. The world continues to become more complex and uncertain. Mollie Rogers Jean De Dieu brings forward a model of leadership that is welcoming and inclusive. I am confident you will benefit from her thoughtful perspective.

Amy C. Edmondson, PhD

Cambridge, Massachusetts, USA

April 2023

Part I

Emotional Inclusion® Defined

'If we start being honest about our pain, our anger, and our shortcomings instead of pretending they don't exist, then maybe we'll leave the world a better place than we found it.'[1]

—Russell Wilson

This is a book from the heart. Not just from mine, but from the eight billion other beating hearts living on planet Earth, who are experiencing what we all are: the school of life. No matter the armours we put up, we are all travellers having a temporary human experience. We are all Emotional creatures who have been wired to feel from the beginning of time that we must not just survive but thrive as well. And yet the greatest irony of all is that we have somehow disregarded the fact that we are human beings who are hardwired to feel—as if, in this 21st century era we live in, we need to remind ourselves that emotions are innate,

---

[1] Howard, Adam (2014, October 3) 'Russell Wilson launches anti-domestic violence campaign: "Pass The Peace"', *MSNBC*, retrieved May 4, 2023, https://www.msnbc.com/msnbc/russell-wilson-launches-anti-domestic-violence-campaign-pass-the-peace-msna426546.

inherited, and deeply primal. In fact, Charles Darwin's early work on the evolution of emotions points out that the emotions of fear, surprise, disgust, happiness, sadness, anger, pride, shame, or embarrassment all developed and adapted over time.

However, stigma around showing emotions lingers. The sad truth is that while we as a species have progressed, showing emotions is still synonymous with being unstable, 'crazy', weak, unprofessional, problematic, and so on. This stands especially true in the corporate landscape, which has remained so unequivocally archaic. I have bathed in it for twenty years now and have heard so many stories of heartbreak from friends, family, and colleagues who have navigated work with their shields up whilst facing the perfect storm. And so have I.

As thought leaders (*and you do not need to be a CEO to be one*), we have the moral obligation to push boundaries in our fields to expand what it means to be human at work. We all have the capacity to change another human being's life, on any given day and no matter the circumstances. We are all contributing members of the community of humankind. I am not just alluding to practising compassion, kindness, or vulnerability. I am also talking about walking our talk, meaningfully and sustainably through laser-focused actions, to really be the change we want to see in this world.

An Objective for All

I felt called to deputize mental health or, as I like to put it, Emotional wellness and unwellness in the workplace, not just because the current approach is so critically outdated, but because the impetus for this timing could not be more needed. In the backdrop of the pandemic, millions of people are leaving their jobs or experiencing some level of stress or anxiety in light of the 'new normal' as they go back to work. When we talk about

Emotional wellness, we need to be clear that caring for our employees equates to caring for our businesses, and ultimately, our global economy. And the snowball effect looks more like an unretractable avalanche than anything else.

As I like to say, the pull is greater than us either way—the companies which choose to ignore this reality will inevitably be left behind. Consider this. 50 per cent of millennials and 81 per cent of Gen Z have left their jobs for mental health reasons[2], and over three in four C-suites allege that the pandemic has negatively affected their Emotional wellness[3]. Today, 68 per cent of employees and 81 per cent of the C-suites say that improving their well-being is more important than advancing their career[4]. The COVID-19 pandemic has furthermore triggered a 25 per cent increase in prevalence of anxiety and depression worldwide[5], resulting in the inevitable increase in absenteeism, turnover, lack of engagement, productivity, etc.

The statistics are as accessible as they are overwhelming. However, this book, I reassure you, is not about giving you statistical data that you yourself can easily access from Google in

---

[2] Greenwood, K., and Anas, J (2021, October 4) 'It's a New Era for Mental Health at Work', *Harvard Business Review*, retrieved February 21, 2023, https://hbr.org/2021/10/its-a-new-era-for-mental-health-at-work.

[3] 'Are leaders supporting wellbeing? It depends on who you ask.', *Insights2Action*, Deloitte, (2022, July 20), retrieved May 4, 2023, https://action.deloitte.com/insight/2388/are-leaders-supporting-wellbeing-it-depends-on-who-you-ask.

[4] Hatfield, S., Fisher, J., and Silverglate, P.H. (2022, June 22) 'The C-suite and workplace wellness', Deloitte, retrieved February 21, 2023, https://www2.deloitte.com/us/en/insights/topics/leadership/employee-wellness-in-the-corporate-workplace.html.

[5] 'COVID-19 pandemic triggers 25% increase in prevalence of anxiety and depression worldwide', World Health Organization, (2022, March 3), retrieved February 21, 2023, https://www.who.int/news/item/02-03-2022-covid-19-pandemic-triggers-25-increase-in-prevalence-of-anxiety-and-depression-worldwide.

a single click. Instead, my aim is to deep-dive into what it means to be emotionally inclusive at work and the bias that still surrounds it. We all want to feel like our lives have value, that our lives and the work that we do are meaningful to our tribe. False stereotypes and biases around emotions in the workplace loom large. We have gotten extremely good at pretending that what we do does not have a huge effect on people, yet today we cannot *not* face this hard truth.

As Albert Einstein articulates so well, 'Our separation from each other is an optical illusion. When something vibrates, the electrons of the entire universe resonate with it. Everything is connected. The greatest tragedy of human experience is the illusion of separateness'.[6] Indeed, the assumption that we are disconnected from each other is still a prevalent undercurrent theme in our society at large. We tend to forget that our humanistic vital needs are, at the core, the same. Dr Tedros Adhanom Ghebreyesus, the World Health Organization Director-General, further addresses the matter by stating that 'the information we have now about the impact of COVID-19 on the world's mental health is just the tip of the iceberg. This is a wake-up call to all companies to pay more attention to Emotional wellness and do a better job of supporting employee mental health'.[7] If you want my straightforward opinion, what we truly need here is a conspiracy of humanness, a full-fledged movement. And whilst I acknowledge that tackling mental health or Emotional wellness in the workplace is no small endeavour, in the words of Martin

---

[6] Einstein, Albert (1950, February 12), 'Letter to Robert S. Marcus', Albert Einstein Archives, The Hebrew University of Jerusalem, https://ein-web. adlibhosting.com/aea/Details/archive/110028196.

[7] 'COVID-19 pandemic triggers 25% increase in prevalence of anxiety and depression worldwide', World Health Organization, (2022, March 2), retrieved February 21, 2023, https://www.who.int/news/item/02-03-2022-covid-19-pandemic-triggers-25-increase-in-prevalence-of-anxiety-and-depression-worldwide.

Luther King Jr., we 'don't have to see the whole staircase, just to take the first step'. And to this I would add: TOGETHER.

Who am I to serve?

I have pondered on this a lot. Now on the outset, I wish to be very clear that I am not writing this book today to preach to you what Emotional inclusion means to me with the aim of convincing you, as that would be all too boring. No, I am writing this book to make us all think a bit more on the definition of Emotional inclusion, contextualize it, and move the needle of Emotional wellness a crank further together. Why? Well, because as Fred Rogers—creator and host of iconic American preschool television series *Mister Rogers' Neighborhood*—put it, 'Anything that's human is mentionable, and anything that is mentionable can be manageable. When we can talk about our feelings, they become less overwhelming, less upsetting, and less scary'.[8] What I am hoping to achieve, then, is for us all to start talking a little more about Emotional wellness at the workplace. How are we going to do that? With Emotional inclusion. We have to stop the narrative that emotions are problematic at the workplace. What this book seeks to do is lift the stigma around talking about Emotional well-being at work and make Emotional inclusion the powerful new status quo.

When I began thinking about the things that defined me most as a female leader, I ended up with a million questions and the most recurrent, loaded one was: who am I to take a stand

---

[8] Rogers, F, as cited by Farmer, D. (2018, September 20), 'What's mentionable is manageable: Why parents should help children name their fears', *The Washington Post*, retrieved February 23, 2023, https://www.washingtonpost.com/news/parenting/wp/2018/09/20/whats-mentionable-is-manageable-why-parents-should-help-kids-name-their-fears/.

on the subject matter of Emotional wellness? After all, I have no relevant qualifications in the realm of psychology. What I do have is a double Bachelor of Arts in Spanish and Italian that has served me absolutely no purpose at all in the part of the world I live in today: Asia. (On the flipside, I am your person if you need a translator whilst on vacation in Italy or Spain.) I was a late bloomer within the realm of academics, but I pulled my weight through the years by learning on terrain and, essentially, learning *with people*. I gravitated to the latter and carved out for myself what some may call a successful career. Struggles harnessed me into coming out stronger, but most importantly, these struggles allowed me to understand the power of human vulnerability.

I am, by nature, a sensitive person and have been brought up, aside from being hardworking and independent, to always be humble, which, oddly enough, is still sometimes socially misperceived as having low self-confidence, which could not be further from the truth. I love how author and organizational psychologist Adam Grant explains this confusion in his book *Think Again*, where he says, 'Humility is often misunderstood. One of the Latin roots of *humility* means "from the earth". It's about being grounded—recognizing that we're flawed and fallible'.[9] And often, humility is born from having experienced suffering; it births in our hearts the understanding that we are not immune to our circumstances.

The point is, I have always been profoundly touched by human suffering throughout my life and have somehow always been a magnet of sorts for those needing to talk. If we make ourselves vulnerable and speak authentically, whilst trying to barrage our way from fear or shyness (the introvert with extrovert qualities speaking here), the depth of our human connections becomes

---

[9] Grant, A. (2021). *Think Again: The Power of Knowing What You Don't Know*, Penguin LCC US.

richer and more meaningful. It then bourgeons into a way of life where 'small talk' becomes almost impossible, or at least, terribly awkward (at least for me).

Real change starts with conscious and educated leadership where the realm of the human, the realm of Emotional inclusion, is front and centre. As Oprah Winfrey puts it, 'So many people live in shame, hiding their struggles, not seeking help. We, as a culture, have not fully acknowledged how much help is needed. The only real shame is on us for not being willing to speak openly. For continuing to deny that mental health is related to overall health. We need to start talking, and we need to start now'.[10] Instead of adopting an imposter syndrome of sorts (which I suspect you might well be familiar with too) within the realm of the Emotional wellness field, I have chosen to act. I am not pretending to have all the solutions or answers, and I am fully cognizant of the fact that 'all roads lead to Rome'. I am a purpose-driven woman and mother who wants to leave this world a better place than I entered it. If my small contribution can help pave the way to allow our children and future generations to be able to show up with their full selves at work, devoid of any questioning or stigma, I would have accomplished my mission and raison d'être.

With almost two decades of being in the retail industry, also known as the industry of people, I have gained a deeper understanding of how the human psyche works and how our behaviours, more often than not, mask the reality we are really living in. There is still so much fear in showing one's real self, especially in the workplace. Yet let me ask you this, when has navigating life through all its ebbs and flows become something we should hide, or worse, be ashamed of? Why are we so intent in perpetuating a robotic approach to business life? Take the

---

[10] Winfrey, O. 'What Oprah Knows for Sure About Mental Illness'. oprah. com, retrieved February 21, 2023, https://www.oprah.com/inspiration/what-oprah-knows-for-sure-about-mental-illness.

example of asking someone you know in the workplace who is going through a hard time how they are feeling. The most common answers will be 'fine', or at the most 'tired', 'stressed', or 'overworked' (or, as the saying goes, 'overworked and underpaid')– while their internal world will be screaming for help, recognition, kindness, a listening ear, and maybe even some non-judgmental guidance. When you ask a female colleague or employee going through a double mastectomy because of breast cancer how she is feeling, to which she responds 'okay', you know that something is awfully wrong with how we perceive the role of emotions in the workplace. The same would apply to when asking a male colleague or employee how he is doing after losing a loved one, for example, to which the same lifeless 'okay' comes up. We give our emotions the backseat and instead choose to live in our silos, opening up to maybe a rare, select few. Yet we are all wired for connection—for which emotions are the gateway to.

I have witnessed or experienced first-hand the dire need for Emotional inclusion throughout my career and life as a whole. What sticks out the most is that we need to clean our 'mental house' to mark any change within this arena. To do this, we ought to look at what our beliefs are about emotions within our society and do a rigorous moral inventory. Let us exercise humility and figure out collectively how we fit into a system that causes so much harm and perpetuates mental and Emotional wellness stigma at work.

At this point, you might be wondering what Emotional inclusion exactly means. In the next section, I will unpack how I coined this term and why I felt called to bring it to the workplace.

The Genesis of Emotional inclusion

As we all know, upping Emotional well-being in the workforce is long overdue and is being run with a lot of outdated information still. It has been hiding behind a curtain of shame and stigma for just too long now. So, whilst we hear about 'mental health' being used left, right, and centre, as a buzzword of sorts, let us perhaps first break down its meaning. Mental health is a state of mental well-being that enables people to cope with the stresses of life, realize their abilities, learn well and work well, and contribute to their community[11]. And whilst we might understand the definition cognitively, we are not being given a handbook per se as to how to tackle mental health issues in real life. To me, *this* is where the catch is.

One key factor determining mental and Emotional wellness at the workplace is Emotional intelligence, which enables us to resolve conflict, coach or motivate others, create a culture of collaboration, and build psychological safety within teams. The term Emotional intelligence, coined by researchers Peter Salavoy and John Mayer in 1990 and popularized by psychologist Daniel Goleman in his 1995 book *Emotional Intelligence*, defines a set of skills hypothesized to contribute to the accurate appraisal and expression of emotion in oneself and in others, the effective regulation of emotion in self and others, and the use of feelings to motivate, plan, and achieve in one's life[12].

But there is, if you ask me, a missing piece integral to the equation: focused, meaningful, sustainable and sensical action. We emote before we even reason. And as such, we need a little bit more than the understanding of what Emotional intelligence means today. Understanding 'why' is not enough, and not focusing on the 'how' through a focused implementation is meaningless. We

---

[11] 'Mental health', World Health Organization, (2022, June 17), retrieved February 21, 2023, https://www.who.int/news-room/fact-sheets/detail/mental-health-strengthening-our-response.

[12] Salovey, P., and Mayer, J.D. (1990, March 1) 'Emotional Intelligence', *Imagination, Cognition and Personality*, 9(3), 185–211, retrieved October, 2022 https://journals.sagepub.com/doi/10.2190/DUGG-P24E-52WK-6CDG.

know the 'why', but as Paul Watzlawick says, 'In psychotherapy, it is the myth of knowing this why as precondition for change which defeats its own purpose.'[13]

Therefore, I coined the term Emotional inclusion. Emotional inclusion is the action of prioritizing the Emotional needs of the workforce in a medical, sustainable, and confidential way. It is about providing tailored mental health care in each company while respecting the organization's DNA, and thereby anchoring a mental health pillar within organizational culture to achieve sustainable change and growth long term.

While Emotional intelligence is all about the knowing of how to navigate our emotions and the emotions of the people we interact with, Emotional inclusion is all about the doing. Inclusion is an action, and it is high time we put our understanding of emotions into a framework that laser-focuses on how to incorporate them into actionable, science-backed ways to see sustainable results in the field of mental and Emotional wellness at work. We must essentially shift gears toward actively respecting the very core of who we are: Emotional creatures.

Emotional inclusion thereby automatically tackles the prevention of Emotional distress and dances, if you will, with psychological safety, which is a coined term popularized by Harvard Business School Novartis Professor of Leadership and Management, Professor Dr Amy C. Edmondson. She defines psychological safety as the belief that one will not be punished or humiliated for speaking up about ideas, questions, concerns, or mistakes, and that interpersonal risk-taking is safe[14]. And as Dr Edmondson

---

[13] Watzlawick, P., Weakland, J.H., and Fisch, R. (1974), *Change: Principles of Problem Formation and Problem Resolution*, Norton, retrieved August, 2022 https://www.abebooks.com/9780393011043/Change-Principles-Problem-Formation-Resolution-0393011046/plp.

[14] Edmondson, A.C., *Psychological Safety – Amy C. Edmondson*, Amy Edmondson, retrieved February 23, 2023, https://amycedmondson.com/psychological-safety/.

acknowledges, 'The organization of the future would be one where the purpose is front and centre, where the culture is healthy and emotionally inclusive'[15]. An author of eight books and widely seen as a pioneer thinker around how psychological safety in the workplace enables enterprise success, Dr Edmondson's validating statement on the integral need for Emotional inclusion in the workplace of the future is nothing short of powerfully significant. As I researched the work done around Diversity, Equity, and Inclusion (DEI) in mostly the larger organizations that could afford to have this 'living' platform, I realized that they spoke of all kinds of DEI themes: cultural, racial, religious, age, sexual and gender diversity, sexual orientation, and disability. My instinctive gut reaction was, *where is Emotional inclusion!*

Chelsea Viñas, a licensed marriage and family therapist and owner of Therapize, a virtual private practice working with women in leadership on impostor syndrome, perfectionism, and trauma, said in an interview that emotions matter because they typically dictate what will come next from us, and 'how you feel about an event will usually lead to your behavior'.[16] You can think about a time when you felt burnt out and disappointed as opposed to one where you felt excited and happy. Your entire day—including your behaviours, how you felt physically and mentally, and your attention—could all be affected by your emotions. The Emotional realm plays a fundamental role in our lives.

Here, it is worth noting that feelings and emotions are not the same. Emotions are subconscious and a physiological response to a stimulus, whilst feelings are a manifestation or expression of felt

---

[15] Edmondson, A.C. (2023) quote as cited by Emotional Inclusion, retrieved February 21, 2023, https://www.emotionalinclusion.com.

[16] Vinas, C. (2022) as cited in Elmer, J. (2022, May 6) 'Why Are Emotions So Important? And How to Address Them', *Psych Central*, retrieved February 21, 2023, from https://psychcentral.com/lib/why-are-feelings-important#why-emotions-matter.

emotions[17]. It is important to know the difference, especially in recent times. It is no newsflash at this point that the COVID-19 pandemic has marked a turning point, moving mental health or Emotional wellness up the list of global health priorities. As countries struggle to rebuild their damaged economies and companies wrestle to recover their losses, they must accept the reality of the financial toll of mental ill-health and invest wisely now. Well-being at work is no longer a 'nice to have' option but a strategic priority to drive the global economy. On the job, accidents and illnesses annually take some two million lives and cost the global economy an estimated US$1.25 trillion[18]. And yet, this pales in comparison to mental 'ill-health', which was estimated to cost the world economy approximately US$2.5 trillion per year in reduced productivity in 2010, a cost projected to rise to US$6 trillion by 2030[19].

A tailored Emotional wellness approach should be our organizational status quo. When we invest in our people, we invest in our business too. Companies are made of people—it is such a matter-of-fact, obvious statement. However, we seem to have forgotten this and instead focus on exploiting our employees to drive their key performance indicators and, by default, even driving some right to their graves. Business Group on Health, an international non-profit that advocates for large employers in health care policy, found that suicide is the second leading cause

---

[17] Fineman, S. (2004, June) 'Getting the Measure of Emotion – and the Cautionary Tale of Emotional Intelligence', *Human Relations*, 57(6), 719–740, https://journals.sagepub.com/doi/10.1177/0018726704044953.

[18] 'Occupational safety and health in times of crisis: "We have to invest in a healthy workforce now"', (2009, November 5), International Labour Organization, retrieved February 21, 2023, https://www.ilo.org/global/about-the-ilo/mission-and-objectives/features/WCMS_116777/lang--en/index.htm.

[19] 'Mental health matters', 2020, November, *The Lancet Global Health*, 8(11), e1352. https://doi.org/10.1016/S2214-109X(20)30432-0.

of death globally for people aged 15–29, and the fifth for those aged 30–49. Approximately 800,000 people commit suicide each year, and many more make suicide attempts[20]. Whilst the causes for these suicide rates are complicated and wide-ranging, let us pause here for a moment and think of these age groups. These are all individuals who are for the most part, just kickstarting their careers.

More data points to the organizational costs of not being emotionally inclusive. While four in ten workers feel burnt out due to factors such as threatened job security, longer work hours, and the need to juggle work and family demands[21], 60 per cent of employees have never spoken to anyone about their mental health[22] and 65 per cent of managers say they could do their jobs more effectively if they found ways to more easily manage distressed employees[23]. All this points to the impact of ignoring Emotional wellness and the large potential opportunity to gain back safe, healthy, productive workplaces by focusing on Emotional inclusion. We simply cannot continue to speak about

---

[20] 'Suicide: An Increasing Concern for Global Employers', Business Group on Health, (2020, Jan 9), retrieved February 21, 2023, https://www.businessgrouphealth.org/resources/suicide-an-increasing-concern-for-global-employers.

[21] 'SHRM Survey: 41 Percent of Workers Feel Burnt Out During Pandemic', (2020, May 11), Society for Human Resource Management, retrieved February 21, 2023, https://www.shrm.org/about-shrm/press-room/press-releases/pages/shrm-survey-41-percent-of-workers-feel-burnt-out-during-pandemic.aspx.

[22] Greenwood, K., Bapat, V., and Maughan, M. (2019, October 7). 'Research: People Want Their Employers to Talk About Mental Health', *Harvard Business Review*, retrieved February 21, 2023, https://hbr.org/2019/10/research-people-want-their-employers-to-talk-about-mental-health.

[23] 'Nine in Ten (91%) Managers and Supervisors Agree It's Important to Improve Their Emotional Intelligence in the Workplace', 2012, Oct 18, Ipsos, retrieved February 21, 2023, https://www.ipsos.com/en-ca/nine-ten-91-managers-and-supervisors-agree-its-important-improve-their-emotional-intelligence.

Emotional wellness at work without getting onto the bandwagon here and doing something about it.

At the beginning of this book, I promised you that it would not be overloaded with statistics (and it will not be), but once you start looking into them, you really get a sense of alarm bells ringing loud and clear. And I will not lie to you, it scares me. But it is also this fear that has pushed me to take the plunge into advocacy of Emotional inclusion.

Taking the Emotional Inclusion Plunge

I had always known that I wanted to make a difference in humanizing the workplace. But as a corporate leader, stepping into my vulnerability, showcasing that it is okay to be vulnerable, took courage. It took me twenty years of corporate life to muster the courage to open my NGO, Emotional inclusion® In the Workplace—a journey I will be sharing with you in further detail in subsequent chapters. I underline the concept of courage because there was so much fear of being 'labelled' looming over me, like a heavy cloud that would not blow away. It took time for me to understand that no endeavour worth undertaking was ever going to be comfortable or easy. I had to put my ego aside.

As Albert Einstein says (yes, I revere the man), 'The intellect has little to do on the road to discovery. There comes a leap in consciousness, call it intuition or what will, the solution comes to you, and you don't know how or why'.[24] My leap of consciousness happened when I just could not take the immense void around Emotional inclusion within the workplace any longer. When I think of how I feel about Emotional inclusion, a popular saying comes to mind: fear can stand for either 'Forget Everything And Run', or 'Face Everything And Rise'. The choice is ours, and I chose the latter.

---

[24] Einstein, A., (April 21, 1997) 'Thoughts on the Business of Life', *Forbes*, retrieved February 23, 2023, https://www.forbes.com/quotes/173/.

In the face of workplace suffering, I opted to 'face everything and rise' because we all go through it at some point in our lives, because it is all around us, and we fail miserably at addressing it on a collective level. Boldly and bravely speaking up to call on measurable action is the only way to spearhead change. The irony is that for most of us (if not all of us perhaps), we are just as afraid of standing out as we are of blending in. As a leader, beyond the fear of failing, I had to dig deep and ask myself the core questions: what is my purpose, what is my value structure, and what are my core beliefs? Why do I get out of bed every morning and why should anyone even care? The peeling of the layers to these questions always circled me back to Emotional inclusion. That unless we validate the humanness in ourselves and in others through tangible actions, we will never make this world a better place. As American motivational author Louise Hay puts it so beautifully, 'Our longing is our calling'.[25] As someone who has always been in touch with her Emotional side, who has felt first-hand what it is like to struggle immensely under the weight of personal and professional circumstances, and who has wished far too many times to be heard, to be better supported in such situations, I felt called to advocate for Emotional wellness in the workplace. How we choose to listen to and act upon our emotions is where I would like us to park our thinking. My mission and purpose are to be a conduit of peace, acceptance, and determined action, about what it means to be human at work, and around what it means to be Emotionally inclusive.

---

[25] Hay, L. (2011, September 1) 'Express Yourself!' HealYourLife.com., retrieved February 23, 2023, https://www.healyourlife.com/express-yourself.

Key Takeaways

- As humans, we are all Emotional creatures who have been wired to feel since birth. The greatest irony of all is that we have somehow disregarded this primal programming in the modern workplace, where showing emotions is seen as unprofessional, weak, and problematic.

- Now, we have the moral obligation to push the boundaries of what it means to be human at work—and to take action. There is no better time than now, amidst the avalanche of change that the pandemic has brought about in the lives of people and in organizations all across the globe. Well-being at work is no longer 'nice to have' but a strategic factor affecting national productivity and economic performance.

- Millions are leaving their jobs due to stress, anxiety, and other mental health issues. Organizations are now awakening to the reality that the mental ill-health of employees translates into financial toll on their bottom lines. Today, caring for employees equates to caring for business. A tailored Emotional wellness approach should be our organizational status quo. Those who choose to ignore this will inevitably be left behind.

- To effect change, we ought to look at what our beliefs are about emotions within our society and do a rigorous take of our moral inventory. When did navigating life through all its ebbs and flows become something we should hide? Why are we so intent in perpetuating a robotic approach to life in the office? We have to stop the narrative that emotions are problematic at the workplace.

- Emotional inclusion is one way to catalyse conversations around Emotional wellness at the workplace. It is the act of prioritizing the psychological needs of the workforce through a medical lens and anchoring a mental and Emotional wellness pillar within organizational culture to achieve sustainable change and long-term growth.
- Inclusion is an action. It is time we put our understanding of emotions into a framework that focuses on how to leverage science-backed methods to see sustainable results in the field of Emotional wellness at work.
- What this book seeks to do is lift the stigma around talking about Emotional wellness at work and make Emotional inclusion the powerful new status quo. By focusing on Emotional inclusion, there is a tremendous potential opportunity to regain safe, healthy, and productive workplaces.

Part II

A New Organizational Platform

'If you change the way you look at things, the things you look at change.'[26]

—WAYNE Dyer

81,396 hours.

As anyone who's held a full-time job will know, we spend most of our lives at work. And 81,396 hours is how long we do it, according to American analytics firm Gallup—making sleep the only thing we do more than work[27]. And how this trickles down and affects our global economic dynamics is chilling. Why, you might ask. Well, because our employees are not doing too well.

---

[26] Dyer, Wayne (2004) *The Power Of Intention: Change The Way You Look At Things And The Things You Look At Will Change*, Hay House.

[27] Clifton, J. (2022, June 14), 'The World's Workplace Is Broken – Here's How to Fix It', Gallup, retrieved February 21, 2023, https://www.gallup.com/workplace/393395/world-workplace-broken-fix.aspx.

Gallup found that 60 per cent of people are emotionally detached at work and 19 per cent are miserable[28].

We have been so conditioned to a workplace devoid of human connection on an Emotional scale that when we try to advocate the normalcy of it, it almost sounds like a foreign novelty to people. And the impetus for this calling could not be more needed than it is today. As John F. Kennedy reminded us, 'Change is the law of life. And those who look only to the past or present are certain to miss the future'.[29] We are habituated to thinking in a certain way, but if we press the pause button for a moment to reflect upon our corporate landscape of today, the proof of how little we have evolved within the workplace since the start of the industrial revolution becomes evident. We still remain profit- and productivity-driven, instead of being people-driven. This is as evident as it is shocking, worrying, upsetting, and, quite frankly, terrifying. Canadian American psychotherapist and writer Nathaniel Branden said, 'The first step toward change is awareness. The second step is acceptance'.[30] And, I think, the third step is sizeable and measurable action, driven through educated thinking and understanding.

The Mind-Body Conundrum

We know that a lot of the data about physical health that insurance companies collect today are actually because of

---

[28] Clifton, J. (2022, June 14), 'The World's Workplace Is Broken – Here's How to Fix It', Gallup, retrieved February 21, 2023, https://www.gallup.com/workplace/393395/world-workplace-broken-fix.aspx.

[29] Kennedy, J. F. (1963, June 25). 'Address in the Assembly Hall at the Paulskirche in Frankfurt (266)', *Public Papers of the Presidents: John F. Kennedy*, JFK Library, retrieved February 21, 2023, https://www.jfklibrary.org/learn/about-jfk/life-of-john-f-kennedy/john-f-kennedy-quotations.

[30] Branden, Nathaniel (1998) *Self-esteem every day: Reflections on self-esteem and spirituality*, Simon and Schuster.

Emotional symptoms. 'Sick days' taken by employees, otherwise known as *absenteeism,* are, more often than not, burn-out days where our levels of exhaustion, stress, and mental fatigue drive us to hibernating under the comfort of our sheets. An estimated twelve billion workdays are lost annually due to depression and anxiety, costing the global economy nearly US$1 trillion[31]. The mind-body connection is not some hippie-fairy, wishy-washy concept. On the contrary, it is backed by undeniable scientific research which proves that our emotions do change our body's physiology. And that the body indeed does keep score[32].

Let us break this down to contextualize this a little further. What this means is that when you are experiencing emotions such as fear, anger, sadness, and stress, it will quite literally alter your physiology too. Studies have observed this phenomenon in actors. When they take on the Emotional states of their characters, their different personalities and behaviours, the *physiology* of their body changes[33]. I don't know about you, but I find this fascinating. What this means is that our Emotional state directly impacts our physical state, and they are correlatively linked. What this depicts is that emotions can significantly affect one's health and well-being. It comes as no surprise, then, that this can have a lasting impact on individuals at work, and cause organizations to lose top performers for good—as was the case with Stephanie.

---

[31] 'WHO and ILO call for new measures to tackle mental health issues at work', World Health Organization, (2022, September 28), retrieved February 21, 2023, https://www.who.int/news/item/28-09-2022-who-and-ilo-call-for-new-measures-to-tackle-mental-health-issues-at-work.

[32] Van der Kolk, B.A. (2015) 'The Body Keeps the Score: Brain, Mind, and Body in the Healing of Trauma', Penguin Publishing Group, https://singapore.kinokuniya.com/bw/9780143127741.

[33] Brown, G.H. (2019), 'Blurred Lines Between Role and Reality: A Phenomenological Study of Acting', AURA—Antioch University Repository and Archive, retrieved February 23, 2023, https://aura.antioch.edu/cgi/viewcontent.cgi?article=1560&context=etds.

Stephanie Dickson, Ex-Events and Marketing Manager at a now defunct Fashion Events Agency

I was fresh out of university and excited about my first foray into the workforce. After completing a double degree in Melbourne and being on lots of committees, I had discovered a passion for events. I had always wanted to work in the fashion industry since I was a little girl. So, when the opportunity to join a fashion events company that planned fashion weeks came up, I jumped at the opportunity.

I joined first as a volunteer and quickly took over to create order and structure to manage all of the fifty volunteers there. After three days I had caught the boss's eye, and he asked me how he could keep me. I felt seen and acknowledged and I worked harder to prove myself more. It was as crazy and magical as I thought it would be. Clothes, celebrities, models, lights, chaos, and so much fun. I joined full-time shortly after and was eager to prove myself.

In the beginning, my boss sung my praises in front of my colleagues, and I was so happy to be in a work environment where my age and experience did not matter—it was how I showed up and what I did now that did. I did not realize that while he was putting me up, he was putting my colleagues—over twenty years my senior—down. This should have been the first, very big red flag, but I was young, eager, and high on the buzz of the glamour and excitement of what we were doing. And he was a master salesman, selling us this epic vision of what we were building for the fashion scene in Singapore and beyond.

Fast forward a few months, and I started to witness more and more of his insane temper, high standards, and abusive nature. It took a while before it got to me, but the verbal abuse, manipulation, and temper tantrums were like nothing I had witnessed before. One time, he threw a chair across the room in anger at my manager, who was also his ex-boyfriend (a very twisted and toxic relationship). Another time, he was so mad he took his laptop and threw it onto a highway.

We all justified the behaviour and let it slide because when you were in his good books, he built you up so much and made you feel so special and capable. But it was only to tear you down next time he was stressed, or something had gone wrong.

The closer we got to a fashion week, the more intense the abuse got. The worst of which was having to go over to his house for a team meeting at 9 p.m. at night after a full day of work, because he was a night owl. We had to work through the night until 6 a.m., with plenty of tantrums and verbal abuses hurled, this time about the website which I was managing. Having never managed a website project before, I had no idea what I was doing or what he wanted, and the brief kept changing. I left there shaking and crying uncontrollably, went home, and attempted to sleep for three hours before waking up to head to work and face him again.

During this period my anxiety reached new heights. I could not sleep. I was on the edge all the time. I checked my phone obsessively to make sure I did not miss any new commands or fires that needed putting out. It was hell.

But I was young, it was my first job, and I did not know better. When the fashion weeks happened, it was so incredible to see what we had built, watch the stunning clothes go down the runway, the glamour of it all, the praise when things went well, I justified to myself that it was worth it.

I lasted four torturous years, during which I became an exemplary employee. I reasoned that if I did not do anything wrong, I would not receive the abuse, right? I learned so much and became excellent at running events and a team (whom I did my best to protect and stand up for, so they did not have to experience what I did). And yet, it was not enough.

We were in Vietnam running a fashion week there when my manager called me up, screaming about the social media account that he knew very well I was not in charge of. It was that moment that the spell I was under shattered, and I realized that it did not matter how good I was—he would always find a reason to try to tear me down, even if it did not have anything to do with me. It was never going to change. So, I decided I was done. I completed the fashion week and quit shortly after.

> *It took me a while to unlearn the stress, anxiety, and tendency to yell when things went wrong. But I was determined not to be like him and to never create a toxic workplace for others. And it took me a while to forgive myself for suffering for so long and be kind and compassionate to myself again.*
>
> *No one should have to tolerate abuse and manipulation in the workplace, which is why Emotional inclusion is important: so that people can feel safe and protected; and that there are checks and opportunities to seek help and support, particularly when mental wellness and health are affected. The more we can normalize Emotional inclusion, the safer workplaces can be, and the more employees can thrive in a supportive environment.*

Stephanie's story demonstrates just how our mental and Emotional states are cornerstones of our health and ability to thrive. Backward, conformist ideologies have us think of the body as being disconnected from the mind. I often enter a tug-of-war in my thinking when I ponder on insurances still mainly covering physical ailments, when these exact ailments, more often than not, have such a profound ripple effect on one's Emotional state. Would not you think that a cancer patient, for example, could also be covered for clinical or sub-clinical depression? I mean, who would not be needing Emotional help in such a distressing time? This issue has only been made all the more apparent after the WHO released a scientific brief in March 2022, outlining the rise in anxiety and depressive disorders at more than 25 per cent during the first year of the pandemic, while also stating that depression is the leading cause of disability[34]. In other

---

[34] 'COVID-19 pandemic triggers 25% increase in prevalence of anxiety and depression worldwide', World Health Organization, retrieved February 21, 2023, https://www.who.int/news/item/02-03-2022-covid-19-pandemic-triggers-25-increase-in-prevalence-of-anxiety-and-depression-worldwide. (2022, March 2).

words, mental health, if left unchecked, can be paralyzing and debilitating. Even more alarming, only 35 per cent of countries reported having national programs for work-related mental health promotion and prevention[35]. What this means is that over six out of ten countries have no plans to provide support or safety nets for those grappling with mental health issues at work. Given the massive costs of ignoring mental health or Emotional wellness on businesses and in turn, the economy—which we discussed earlier—it makes little sense for nations to ignore this workplace health crisis. I mean, hello? Someone there? Knock-knock?

The question still lingers as to how and why the health of our employees has deteriorated so drastically over the years to reach the global crisis mode it is in now. And why it is that we have not made more substantial progress in this arena. It remains crucial, I believe, to go back to the Industrial Revolution to understand the role it played in its deterioration of working conditions. Let us dive deep into how our quest for profit overshadowed the wellness and safety of people, how so shockingly little has changed since, and where we are at today.

A Continuous Neglect

The industrial revolution began in the 18th century[36], and transformed our previously agricultural societies into industrial and urban ones. It was a technological, socioeconomic, and cultural transformation that marked tremendous advancements, but also left mental health or Emotional wellness as open wounds well into the 21st century. What do I mean by this? The industrial revolution did not just bring about the usage of new energy

---

[35] 'Mental Health Atlas 2020', 2021, World Health Organization. https://www.who.int/publications/i/item/9789240036703.

[36] 'Industrial Revolution', HISTORY.com, retrieved March 14, 2023, https://www.history.com/topics/industrial-revolution.

sources or the invention of new machines, it also brought forth a new organization of work, known as factories. These factories consisted of once rural workers, who used to work with their tools and materials, and set their own hours of work. In the quest for mass production to incentivize profits, factories quickly became inadequate quarters where workers were cramped in and overworked. Trauma from machinery, toxic and unsanitary conditions, minimal breaks, and low remunerations were all disregarded[37].

While I am not negating the positive changes in innovation and production that came with the industrial revolution, I am spelling out here the deplorable working conditions that stemmed from it and that have, in many ways, not been completely erased from our workplace psyche. These poor workplace practices gave rise to trade union movements in the 19th century where workers called for fairer circumstances, yet it really was not until the 20th century that healthier working conditions were officially required by government regulations. Yet, these fairer regulations were more centred around the factories than the workers themselves. The improvements mainly centred around better lit premises, sounder ventilation, and more automated machines, which eased the production chain and the workload strain[38].

Fast forward two centuries post the industrial revolution, and the narrative behind promoting healthier and safer workplaces for all remains a very relevant and dire subject matter. The advancements made have been microscopic, and the evidence is screamingly obvious. According to the World Health Organization,

---

[37] 'The Industrial Revolution. The Evolution of Epidemiologic Thinking', Boston University School of Public Health, retrieved March 14, 2023, https://sphweb.bumc.bu.edu/otlt/mph-modules/ep/ep713_history/ep713_history4.html.

[38] 'Factory system', Encyclopedia Britannica, retrieved March 14, 2023, https://www.britannica.com/topic/factory-system.

3.5 billion people worldwide are workers, yet two million deaths from unsafe work occur every year[39]. Whether it be focused on work-related diseases or injuries, the focus on caring for the welfare of our employees still calls for urgent action. This begs for governmental, organizational, and personal introspection. The fact that we are still having to address the matter clearly spells out how little we have learned in the span of 200 years, and how very inefficiently we have properly addressed the humanity of the individuals we employ. There is no question that it has yielded economic progress. However, the impacts of our dysfunctional workplaces call for a new approach: a global, action-driven commitment toward institutionalizing a preventative approach towards wellness within our organizations today.

It was not until June 2022[40] that the International Labour Conference decided to amend paragraph 2 of the ILO Declaration on Fundamental Principles and Rights at Work, first penned in 1998, to call for the inclusion of 'a safe and healthy working environment at work' in the International Labour Organization's agenda. In the declaration, the organization proclaimed a safe and healthy working environment as a fundamental principle and right and said that it affirms the obligation and commitment of governments, employers and workers alike, to eradicate forced or compulsory labour, child labour, discriminations of employment and occupation, and promotes a safe and healthy working environment. Whilst this amendment is no doubt a clear message of willingness to address the future of our workplaces, how

---

[39] 'Promoting healthy, safe and resilient workplaces for all', World Health Organization, retrieved March 14, 2023, https://www.who.int/activities/promoting-healthy-safe-and-resilient-workplaces-for-all.

[40] 'ILO Declaration on Fundamental Principles and Rights at Work', International Labour Organization, retrieved March 14, 2023, https://www.ilo.org/declaration/lang--en/index.htm.

effectively it trickles down into each and everyone's agenda will be left to be seen. My hope is that we will not have to wait another century or two to witness beneficial changes within this realm. As the old adage goes, actions speak louder than words, and I trust you will agree that inaction speaks volumes either way.

Time for Action

Raising awareness around taking measurable action is a fundamental pillar of inclusion. Raising awareness around taking measurable *Emotional wellness action* is a fundamental pillar of *Emotional inclusion.*

Objectively, it is only when we begin to take stock of our surroundings, of the negative consequences certain belief structures have on our welfare and well-being, that we start to question said beliefs. I think it is fair to say that we have all bathed in the blindfolded acceptance of our backwards and dysfunctional workplace landscape. The so-called hamster wheel of office life has been in hyperdrive for too long. The pandemic has, to some measure, shaken things up, awakened mass consciousness in such a way that people no longer want to accept being treated like machines. Sure, we have spoken of work-life balance for decades now; however, work-life balance can only truly work if companies help their employees in this endeavour. It is no assumption that employees want to be a part of something bigger, they want to make a difference and get behind something that they believe in. This is true, now more than ever.

Recently, in response to growing disillusionment around work, companies have begun to define their purpose and explore how people, planet, and profit can all coexist. Yet how this translates throughout the workplace remains fractured and inconsistent. Whether through corporate social responsibility, environmental, social, and governance efforts, sustainability platforms, DE&I departments—which still mostly exist in larger companies for now—or Chief Sustainability Officers, who are being hired to drive cultural change, every company acts upon its purpose differently. This causes confusion, not only to existing employees and potential recruits, but also to the organization itself, which ends up being confused about what it needs to explicitly put into practice.

The fact of the matter is that there are too many damaging office practices. On one hand, companies may preach about wellness at work. And on the other they will perpetuate the mindset that staff are not performing unless they are racing through their days, meeting impossible deadlines, or answering every email that comes their way as quickly as they can. There is no question that the workplace wellness barometer takes a plunge in this scenario. And so, I beg to ask, why are we not reframing our organizational beliefs in such a way that we can stop perpetuating unhealthy workplace habits? We know that ignoring employees' mental wellness leads to unhappiness, dissatisfaction, and, ultimately, lower productivity and higher turnover. Would you honestly tell a doctor to speed her or his way through caring for a patient? The obvious answer is no. So why would we pressurize our employees to work at breakneck speeds, when we know that it will impact their wellness and performance? Could we not look at slowness as an asset and equate it to quality and thoroughness of work instead? There is really no contouring the obvious truth: companies that operate without their workforce in mind are the ones that perpetuate emotional toxicity and negative workplace culture.

A Need for Change

There is no question in my mind that there is a need for strong winds of change to blow through our dusty and spiderweb-ridden workplace. For the sake of our children and future generations, we must start passing down workplace wisdom instead of workplace wounds. One can clearly see how little advancement we have made over time, and how much there is still to be done in the arena of Emotional inclusion. I will acquiesce that it is neither an easy nor a straightforward subject matter to tackle. Yet it remains our ethical responsibility.

We must ask ourselves the right questions as a collective to mark change for good. The word *cure* comes from the word *curious*[41]. If only we could keep our inquisitive minds open enough, then surely, we will find the healing antidote to our sick work landscape. Yet finding a cure through curiosity is perhaps not enough, if we cannot be candid about our emotions. We are all coping with the stresses of life and all of us have, at some point or another, experienced its impact on our mental health (a safe assumption to make, wouldn't you say?). Emotional exposure equates to being vulnerable, and unlearning the heavy load of bias the world carries. The fear of vulnerability, especially in the workplace, looms large. Yet American professor Brené Brown, whose research revolves around vulnerability, says being vulnerable fosters authenticity, belonging, and love[42].

How vulnerability shows up in our everyday lives at work is through talking about mistakes that we might have made, taking a chance that might lead to a rejection, sharing personal information that we would have kept quiet on before, and speaking up about things that bother us, versus bottling them up and ignoring them. In other words, opening up is the starting step in our journey to building better workplaces. But here is the catch: there cannot be Emotional exposure without Emotional inclusion. Unless we

---

[41] 'Curious Definition & Meaning', Merriam-Webster, retrieved March 14, 2023, https://www.merriam-webster.com/dictionary/curious.

[42] Brown, B. (2012), *Daring Greatly*, Penguin Publishing Group.

harbour workplace cultures that actively encourage employees to speak up with no fear, that actively endorse humanity and fallibility, then, let us face it, very few will take the leap. The ramifications of not speaking up will mean that employees will not receive the care, support, or protection they might need.

If the days of not talking about mental health are gone, then surely, the days of not talking about Emotional inclusion should be too. On an Emotional wellness advocacy front, it is now increasingly common and recognized to offer employee assistance programmes, mental health self-assessment tools and portals, free or subsidized clinical screenings for depression and mental well-being coaches etc. Yet on an emotionally inclusive front, what are companies doing to harbour the humanity of their employees at the most primal level? In other words, what are companies doing to erase the outdated concept of the 'work persona' and instead encourage employees to show up as their full selves at work, with authenticity and vulnerability? What are companies doing to harbour deep, humanistic connection? What are companies doing to encourage Emotional trust and emotionally inclusive cultures? The answer to this is, sadly, acutely evident: very little.

To create *emotionally inclusive cultures,* we must first identify which negative emotions are the most prevalent at work, and which ones are the top-rated ones, so as to take long-term, educated action—let us remember here that inclusion is an action. According to employee engagement firm Quantum Workplace, negative emotions include anxiety, boredom, disinterest, dissatisfaction, frustration, gloominess, miserableness, sadness, stress, tiredness, uncomfortableness, unhappiness, upsettedness, and worry[43]. Their research found that the top negative emotions in the workplace, as rated by employees, are the following:

---

[43] Stange, J. (2021, January 21), 'Emotion with the Workplace: How to Deal with Emotions at Work', *Quantum Workplace*, retrieved March 15, 2023, from https://www.quantumworkplace.com/future-of-work/emotions-in-the-workplace-how-to-deal-with-emotions-at-work.

- Frustration (56.2 per cent)
- Stress (45.1 per cent)
- Anxiety (30.4 per cent)

I invite us all to pause right here for a moment. Surely, we can all remember times when we experienced these emotions at work. And for most of us, when we felt these emotions, we had no choice but to suck it up—to speak crudely yet truthfully—and put on a façade. Yet the irony in this fear-based coping behaviour is that avoiding our emotions is simply impossible, be it at home or at work. Accepting that our emotions are a natural part of our makeup is crucial.

Second in the path to an emotionally inclusive culture is acknowledging that ignoring our emotions is really damaging to our mental health. Now, this is not some 'woo-woo', baseless statement. According to recent clinical, social, and health psychology research, individuals who allow themselves to label their emotions are less prone to resorting to binge drinking, self-harm, aggression, depressive, or anxious states[44]. Debunking the myth that emotions do not belong in the workplace is, once again, passé. So yes, practising Emotional awareness is crucial, yet how we act upon this Emotional awareness is ultimately what builds an emotionally inclusive culture.

Although some companies simply skirt around the issue of workplace wellness, neglecting Emotional inclusion at work has concrete consequences. The largest surveys of the global workforce conducted in 2022 found that one in five workers planned to quit their job, with a third citing the desire for greater

[44] Kashdan, T.B., Feldman Barrett, L., & McKnight, P.E. (2015, February 18), 'Unpacking Emotion Differentiation: Transforming Unpleasant Experience by Perceiving Distinctions in Negativity', *Current Directions in Psychological Science*, 24(1), 10–16, retrieved August, 2022 https://journals.sagepub.com/doi/abs/10.1177/0963721414550708.

fulfilment[45]. Hang on. Does not more fulfilment start with more psychological safety and Emotional inclusion? When employees are in a safe ecosystem that is emotionally inclusive, they do not have to deal with the frustrations of hiding their pain or the complications of their personal lives from the office. Knowing that they can show up fully, that they do not have to hide behind a façade, leaves people feeling more fulfilled in knowing that they are seen for who they are and are accepted.

When we talk about mental health or Emotional wellness, it is very important we be clear and make no distinction between caring for our employees and caring for our businesses at large. These two go hand in hand. People are what make our companies, not the other way around. It is such a basic concept that it utterly baffles me that more companies are not walking their talk more actively and pressingly, when it comes to caring for the humanity of the individuals they lead.

Every single time I deliver an Emotional inclusion keynote to companies, I get employees coming up to me at the end of my talk to tell me how relevant this subject matter is and how they wished Emotional inclusion could be the status quo in their companies. They inquire about the Emotional inclusion programme we offer and always, in a hushed voice, ask me to do whatever I can to onboard it in their organization. Many of these individuals share with me their stories of hardship at work and how they feel so powerless in not being able to voice out how they truly feel. These are always goosebump-inducing moments, where vulnerability takes centre stage. I will always remember this one person who shared with me his struggle with depression after having had a colleague he befriended at work commit suicide during the pandemic. He recounted his journey of complete shock

---

[45] 'PWC's Global Workforce Hopes and Fears Survey 2022', 2022, May 24, PWC, retrieved February 21, 2023, https://www.pwc.com/gx/en/issues/workforce/hopes-and-fears-2022.html.

and disbelief in how it was handled at a company level. How the incident was left unaddressed with employees, and how the company coped with it in a hush-hush manner. To this day, this story deeply strikes a chord with me. The only way we will get to making Emotional inclusion the new status quo in the workplace is through the recognition that change is required. As Elon Musk put it, 'Some people don't like change, but you need to embrace change if the alternative is disaster'.[46] The alternative to not taking a serious medical and professional approach to Emotional wellness in our organizations today is disaster. People are burnt out and fed up with an outdated workplace model requiring them to sit at their computers from 9 a.m. to 6 p.m.—or, for most of us, much longer than that—and plug away at schedules filled to the brim with back-to-back meetings while putting on a front and ignoring their personal pain, whether that be the pain of losing a loved one, going through marital issues, navigating critical illnesses, experiencing financial struggle, or whatever other hardship life might throw their way.

New Ways Moving Forward

We have just undergone a global mass trauma, one that will go down in history books, one that will remain stained on our psyches for decades. And COVID-19 continues to take a toll on the collective mental health of our society at large: people who have lost loved ones, contracted the virus, or worked on the front lines continue to be at greater risk for developing post-traumatic stress. The reality, as we all know, is that we were vastly unprepared for the damaging ramifications COVID-19 has, and

---

[46] Musk, E. (2022, June 26) as cited by 'Inc. in 51 Elon Musk Quotes Ranked in Order of Pure Elon Muskiness'. Inc.com, retrieved February 21, 2023, https://www.inc.com/bill-murphy-jr/51-elon-musk-quotes-ranked-in-order-of-pure-elon-muskiness.html.

continues to have, on our mental health. To add to the equation, we are still motioning with a massive shortage of mental health resources. In 2020, governments worldwide spent an average of just 2 per cent of health budgets on mental health, with lower-middle income countries investing less than 1 per cent[47].

We are all scrambling as a result. We have too few psychologists, too few focused preventative treatment plans, too few evidence-based mental health or Emotional wellness libraries, and so on. What this means is fewer professionals to study our psyche and understand how our thoughts control our lives, a too-small body of case studies and research on the benefits of therapy and the link between therapy and wellness, and less therapy available to all. Nations are not placing the attention or budgets they should on Emotional wellness. By doing that, they are shooting themselves in the foot because mental wellness affects productivity, which in turn affects profitability, industry, and entire economies.

You may wonder how exactly mental and Emotional wellness affect productivity. Social and Emotional exclusion, like the kind we experienced during the pandemic, is a psychologically painful experience. Neuroscience research shows that being left out of social circles lights up the same areas of the brain as the experience of physical pain[48]. And this pain is being experienced by the people who have lost loved ones, contracted COVID-19, or worked on the front lines, and are now struggling with depression or related illnesses. Many, lacking the tools and strength necessary

---

[47] 'WHO and ILO call for new measures to tackle mental health issues at work', World Health Organization, (2022, September 28), retrieved February 21, 2023, https://www.who.int/news/item/28-09-2022-who-and-ilo-call-for-new-measures-to-tackle-mental-health-issues-at-work.

[48] O'Reilly, J., & Banki, S. (2016) 'Research in Work and Organizational Psychology: Social Exclusion in the Workplace', *Social Exclusion: Psychological Approaches to Understanding and Reducing Its Impact* (pp. 133–155), Springer, retrieved February, 2023 https://www.researchgate.net/publication/305673487_Research_in_Work_and_Organizational_Psychology_Social_Exclusion_in_the_Workplace.

to tackle these issues and afraid of others' judgement, have withdrawn into themselves and chosen to isolate themselves from others. Spending most of their energy just trying to survive each day, it is little wonder they are less productive. It is critical that employers create an emotionally inclusive and informed workplace, whether employees are returning to the office or remaining remote. The more we enable people to speak up about their emotions and acknowledge the mind–body connection, the more Emotional inclusion can take place, and the more both workers and organizations can benefit.

How may this look like in practical terms? Well, how about considering, first and foremost, our existing DEI platforms, and what could be done there? One suggestion would be to add Emotional inclusion as part of the job scope of chief diversity officers of companies. It would be a clear key performance indicator that these officers would be evaluated on yearly. The idea would be for them to foster a detailed plan of action of what Emotional inclusion would look like within the context of their company culture and their company targets within the said arena. Strategies would, of course, be varied, but they could, for example, be about making it an official guideline to kick off the start of each meeting by asking each employee to name one or two emotions that they are feeling that given day, or that they are feeling in the moment, without necessarily having to explain the details. This acts as an Emotional barometer of sorts to understand where everyone in the room is at, it creates space for more empathy, and ultimately steers the meeting in a more meaningful manner.

For me, there is no question that Emotional inclusion should be integrated in all DEI programmes as part of companies' firm stand in taking tailored and sustainable action in this domain. Diversity, Equity, and Inclusion, three interlinked values, work together to emphasize meaningful progress in the awareness of race, ethnicity, age, gender, sexual orientation, physical ability, and neurodiversity. Yet notice that the awareness of emotions, which is vital to our Emotional well-being and mental health, does NOT figure in the DEI list of priorities as it stands today. Moreover, what DEI platforms do is contextualize new ways of thinking to shift mindsets, behaviours, and practices. Emotional intelligence, by obvious deduction, is a key building block in creating a successful DEI platform[49]. If we break this all down, then, if Emotional intelligence is a key component of DEI platforms, and if Emotional intelligence is all about the *knowing* of how to navigate our emotions and the emotions of the people we interact with, then where does the action bit come into play? Inclusion refers to 'the act or practice of including and accommodating people who have historically been excluded'[50]. So, what Emotional inclusion does is put Emotional intelligence into action, by taking measurable and sustainable steps towards caring for the Emotional realms of individuals. We could perhaps think of Emotional inclusion as the driver of Emotional intelligence. Emotional Intelligence might give you the ability to perceive or at best understand someone's pain, but Emotional inclusion will drive you to get the help you need, medically and confidentially.

The path toward mental wellness at the workplace is not a straightforward one. As I sit in meetings with other CEOs and we discuss pragmatic, sensible, realistic, and measurable ways to tackle making Emotional wellness a foundational pillar in our organizations, I am continuously surprised at the lack of structured focus there is around the topic. Firstly, there are the CEOs who

---

[49] 'How Emotional Intelligence Drives Organizational DEI Initiatives and Creates Psychological Safety', (2022, February 9), Institute for Health and Human Potential, retrieved March 15, 2023, https://www.ihhp.com/blog/2022/02/09/how-emotional-intelligence-drives-organizational-dei-initiatives/.

[50] 'Inclusion Definition & Meaning',. Merriam-Webster, retrieved March 15, 2023, https://www.merriam-webster.com/dictionary/inclusion.

are half-hearted about tackling Emotional wellness, who put in inadequate and superficial measures such as wellness retreats or mental health hotlines or apps—or worse, none at all—that do little to seriously tackle the issue of Emotional inclusion. Then there are the CEOs who are serious about ensuring that their mental health or Emotional wellness measures are robust, and who dedicate substantial budgets to seeking long-term solutions. Yet even this second group suffers from a lack of direction as to where to go from there to bring about real Emotional inclusion.

Meditation or sleeping apps and 24/7 hotlines are what I call 'crutches'. They are nice to have. They are, at the very least, something. But one thing they are not is sustainable. Think of it: how do you integrate them into your company to see quantifiable results? One answer could come from the recently updated global guidelines on mental health at work, issued by the World Health Organization and the International Labour Organization, to frame a collective strategy. These guidelines, called the Comprehensive Mental Health Action Plan 2013–2030, comprise recommendations for action around the following four key objectives:

1. **Stronger effective leadership and governance.** For example, senior business leaders can speak up on mental health and work to instil a stigma-free culture in organizations.
2. **Comprehensive, integrated, and responsive community-based care.** To do this, organizations can create mental wellness departments staffed by accredited psychologists and develop tailored support plans for employees.
3. **Strategies for promotion and prevention.** For example, running storytelling campaigns to enhance the normalcy of talking about mental health issues at the workplace.

4. **Stronger information systems, evidence, and research.** For example, companies can refer to guidelines from the World Health Organization and other major institutions, and partner with mental health advocacy platforms as they deepen their understanding of mental health.

This is a powerful line-up of communal tactical implementations and proves that where there is Emotional wellness action, there will be Emotional inclusion.

Speaking of a structured approach to facilitating Emotional wellness at the workplace, one other area that organizations can tap in to benefit employees in a very significant way is through insurance. Cognizant of a new mental health or Emotional wellness wave, insurers are reinventing themselves urgently to keep up with the changing focus, even as they grapple with the costs of integrating mental healthcare benefits. Take the insurance group AXA, for example. They, alongside organizations such as The Mental Health + Work Design Lab at Columbia University, have developed a 'Mental Health at Work Index', which is a scorecard allowing companies to evaluate their wellness barometer. This score 'provides a data-driven assessment and generates strategic guidance for improvement in key organizational categories that are foundational and closely linked to mental health'.[51] I look forward to seeing the impact new initiatives such as these will have on companies, and the world.

Paving the way to a more holistic and humanistic Emotional wellness ecosystem in the workplace is no easy feat, yet we are called to contribute for the greater good. It is undeniable that we all have the moral obligation to make emotionally inclusive

---

[51] 'Introducing the Mental Health at Work Index™', Mental Health at Work Index, retrieved February 23, 2023, https://mentalhealthindex.org.

mental health or Emotional wellness practices in the workforce sustainable, confidential, and medicalized. We all have the moral obligation to practice constant awareness around caring for our employees because if we do that, it will inevitably affect our business for the better. I love Maya Angelou's quote where she says 'If you don't like something, change it. If you can't change it, change your attitude'.[52] This is what I am calling on all CEOs and global movers and shakers to look at—with a business eagle eye, but also with an open heart. This is the case that I will be continuing to militate for in succeeding chapters too.

Key Takeaways

- We have been so conditioned to a workplace devoid of human connection that advocating for emotions to have a seat at the table is a foreign concept—even a novelty—for many. The corporate workplace of today has evolved little since the start of the Industrial Revolution, and we still remain profit- and productivity-driven, instead of being people-driven. Churning out as much as possible, no matter what it takes to achieve this goal, including the wellness and safety of our people, has been the unquestioned status quo.
- Research has clearly shown the link between our physical health and Emotional state. The pandemic awakened a mass consciousness about this and people no longer want to accept being treated like machines. Employees seek a safe environment that is emotionally inclusive,

---

[52] Angelou, M., as cited in 'Maya Angelou: In her own words', *BBC*, (2014, May 28), retrieved February 23, 2023, https://www.bbc.com/news/world-us-canada-27610770.

where they no longer have the additional burden of hiding the pain and suffering from the other parts of their lives at the office. On the flipside, not taking a serious, medicalized, and professional approach to Emotional wellness in our companies today will result in organizational disaster. COVID-19 has resulted in a global mass trauma that will remain stained in our psyches for decades: people have lost loved ones, suffered from poor health, endured financial stress, and been severely overworked in mentally taxing environments.

- Mental wellness affects productivity, which in turn affects profitability, industry, and entire economies. The more we enable people to speak up about their emotions and acknowledge the mind-body connection, the more Emotional inclusion can take place, and the more both workers and organizations can benefit. Emotional inclusion should be integrated in all organizations' Diversity, Equality, and Inclusion (DEI) programmes, and tailored and sustainable plans should be created specifically for this pillar.

- The path toward mental wellness at the workplace is not a straightforward one. It is rife with surface-level fixes, such as Emotional wellness apps, wellness retreats, and 24/7 hotlines. Leaders, even well-meaning ones, lack direction as to how to bring about true Emotional inclusion. It is encouraging that, organizations and companies such as insurers are stepping up by creating organizational guidelines and strategic guidance tools to improve the evaluation and promotion of workplace Emotional wellness.

- We have a moral obligation to make Emotional wellness practices in the workforce sustainable and inclusive. Paving the way for a more accepting Emotional wellness ecosystem in the workplace is no easy feat. It is a matter that leaders in particular should take a call on with a heightened sense of responsibility.

Part III

The Stigma

'One does not become fully human painlessly.'[53]

—ROLLO MAY

Let us face it: we still live in a weak, watered-down mediocre society, where emotions are still recognized very little, almost as if the truth that lies behind our humanness is one that we should be ashamed of. No one would ever dare say to, say a COVID patient, to 'just get over it'. Why people allow themselves to do that to those with Emotional struggles shocks me to no extent.

The core issue here is that showing emotion is not 'safe' to do. It has been stigmatized and subjects us to the judgment of others. It is riddled with negative labels that we simply do not want to have to confront. What is stigma? The Cambridge dictionary defines it as a 'strong feeling of disapproval that most people in society have about something'[54]. And how this plays out

---

[53] May, Rollo (1978) Foreword to *Existential-Phenomenological Alternatives for Psychology*, by Ronald S. Valle and Mark King, Oxford University Press.

[54] 'Stigma', Cambridge Dictionary, retrieved February 22, 2023, https://dictionary.cambridge.org/dictionary/english/stigma.

in a performance-driven workplace is people acting robotically even as they grapple with suffering, having to put a smile on their faces, and appear upbeat and positive at all times, for fear of being judged or dismissed otherwise. Stigmas act as brakes for Emotional inclusion and impede employees from being accepted and respected for being humane.

Showing up at work as our full selves on difficult days and being able to 'not be okay' should no longer be viewed as a sign of weakness or unprofessionalism. It is well overdue that we max up our humanity in all arenas of our life. It is time to crank up the dial to mega high. In the shadow of the pandemic, we must be brave with our human intimacy. Intimacy, you might you ask? Yes, as improvisational comedy teacher Martin de Maat said, 'You know what intimacy is? It's into-me-you-see'. And this begs the question: when did we stop being more understanding, more accepting of ourselves and others?

Emotional inclusion invites others to look into our humanness. Being emotionally inclusive means being emotionally and mutually accepting of one another, so much so that a more open, understanding, and accommodating environment of trust can and will be cultivated. It is acknowledging that no emotion is good or bad, that they are part of our integral biological make-up, thereby enabling us to pilot our way through life. Failing to do so can lead to various forms of escapism, such as falling into vices, alongside possible physical and mental ailments like depression.

An Aversion to Emotion

All that suppressing of our emotions really does is lead to far more damage than we wish to look at. We should not deaden our emotions, as they are messengers which invite us to look at exactly what needs healing, softness, and compassion. They are there to be heard and to be addressed. And if you ask me, gently and compassionately catching ourselves in the midst of fear, doubt, and pain should be the path of the corporate Emotional wellness warrior. This change in perception will take time, but, as we have discussed thus far in previous chapters and will continue to do so in succeeding ones, the benefits far outweigh the drawbacks.

Brandon's story below is one such example that illustrates just how damaging stigma can be if workers withdraw and do not feel comfortable speaking up.

Brandon Tey, Former Banker, now a Therapist in the Social Service Sector

After spending fourteen years working for a technology vendor selling enterprise IT solutions to governments, telecoms operators, and banks, I decided to take on a new challenge by joining a bank. Having worked with banks for a few years, supporting them with various projects, I thought I knew how banks operate and was confident I could do the job.

However, the reality proved to be the complete opposite and I soon found myself struggling to adapt. With my background of twenty years' working experience, I was appointed as a Vice President and there were only a handful of colleagues with the same job title within the team. A few weeks into the job, I realized there was a lot about banking operations, processes, and technology that I did not know. I was not familiar with the technologies the bank had adopted, how things needed to be done a certain way due to banking regulations, and, in general, the processes within the bank.

I was overwhelmed, as it was increasingly challenging to navigate my way within this large organization. And to make things worse, I began to compare myself to other team members. I felt that many of them appeared capable, confident, and were able to cope with their work with no difficulty. It did not help that most of them were younger, which made me feel inadequate and incompetent in comparison.

I started to feel embarrassed and ashamed of myself and lost my self-confidence at work. I did not feel that I deserved the job title that I was being offered and began feeling more anxious and fearful of being seen as someone who could not perform well.

I started to spiral downwards. I began feeling extreme anxiety at work. My heart would pump very fast, and I found myself having trouble thinking straight and remembering things, as if there was a blockage in my brain. When my anxiety got too overwhelming, I had to be alone by hiding in the toilet cubicle, just to take time to calm myself down. I was also fearful that my colleagues would notice my struggle and felt more and more pressured to perform well, be productive, and live up to my job title.

Despite these work struggles, I resisted asking others for help because I did not want them to think I was not as capable as they had thought, that I was an 'imposter' who did not deserve my job title at work.

Naturally, I felt afraid of attending meetings in case I had to share my work progress or was asked to share my opinion about any topic being discussed, worrying people would discover my incapability. So whenever I attended meetings, I would sit in a corner, hoping no one would notice me.

I vividly recalled that during one meeting, my boss told everyone, 'If the product you're managing is crap, it's your fault!' Hearing that sent a shiver down my spine. I feared that it would soon be obvious I was struggling since it would show up in my poor work performance. And people would eventually realize I was not as capable as they had thought. It was impossible to put up a pretence, and that thought scared the hell out of me!

The continued anxiety began affecting my sleep and appetite. I would feel drained and tired each day I reached home from work and would head to bed after a quick dinner. But I had trouble getting a good night's rest and struggled to stay asleep for more than 2–3 hours each night. I would wake up in fear, worrying about how things would turn out for me the next day at work, and could only lie in bed wide awake for the next 4–5 hours, until I had to wake up at 6 a.m. in the morning.

It seemed like no one in my office noticed my struggle. Everyone was busy with their own projects and meeting their individual KPIs. I did not have the courage to share this with anyone as I did not want to be perceived as weak, incapable, or unable to cope with stress. Being in this situation made me feel ashamed of myself. I wanted to maintain a social image by pretending that everything was okay. I continued to maintain a low profile in order to not get noticed.

I was in distress and could only live one day at a time, trying my best to cope with the anxiety and fear. It got to a point that I found myself wishing I could get into a car accident to have a valid reason to excuse myself from work. At that point, I knew I needed help.

I made an appointment to visit a psychiatrist and he diagnosed me with General Anxiety Disorder. He gave me some medication and sleeping pills to help me with my sleep. Together with counselling, I gradually recovered from it. The counsellor helped me to identify some of the unhelpful beliefs that got me stuck in that unhelpful pattern of anxiety and fear.

This experience served as a powerful reminder of how societal norms and stigmas can inadvertently exert tremendous pressure on individuals. It is a common tendency for people to be obliged to project a brave and composed persona, even in the face of personal struggles. This, in turn, can lead to a pervasive sense of inadequacy, imposter syndrome, and anxiety. However, I feel grateful for this experience as it has shown me the importance of seeking help and not allowing societal pressures to govern my emotions or actions.

It highlighted the importance of recognizing and addressing the impact of societal expectations and stigma on mental health, the importance of seeking help and support when needed, and the power of vulnerability and authenticity in promoting Emotional inclusion in the workplace. By embracing these principles, companies can create a culture that prioritizes Emotional inclusion and mental well-being and supports their employees in achieving their full potential.

As Brandon's story depicts so clearly, the ramification of today's hustle culture perpetuates a stigma around failing to keep up with the unrealistic, robotic, and destructive pace of work. The shame associated with this behavioural stigma or the discrimination and prejudice that goes along with it should raise big red flags to employers. Yet, you would be surprised how desensitized employers are globally. According to a Health Employer 2020 Survey led by McKinsey, reducing stigma came at the bottom of the 2021 priority list for employers, even though 75 per cent of these same employers admitted the existence of stigma in their companies[55]. Whilst tackling stigma can be too conceptually daunting to address head-on, it is the very source of our 21st century organizational mental health or Emotional wellness woes. You might perhaps be wondering: then, what are employers' priorities? Well, the top ones are the same ones we hear about from pretty much across the board: productivity, engagement, mental health treatment, reducing burnout, tackling well-being, stress, anxiety, improving mental health literacy, etc. Sound familiar? I thought they would. Does it feel detached and surface-level to you too?

As established in the previous chapter, sick days might as well be called 'burnout days', and the mind–body connection is undeniable when it comes to discussing mental health or Emotional wellness holistically. Whilst so little change has taken place in the arena of mental health throughout the centuries, I would vigorously argue that there is an urgency to look at stigma as the gateway to creating emotionally inclusive workplace cultures.

Emotional inclusion invites us to change the core of our discriminating attitude and false assumptions when labelling each other's humanity. This is exactly how stigma silently plays out in the workplace. The hyper-focus on profit and productivity casts shame or judgment on anyone who fails to deliver. There is something deadly wrong in how we can still allow ourselves

---

[55] Coe, E., Cordina, J., Enomoto, K., & Seshan, N. (2021, July 23), 'The battle against mental-health stigma', McKinsey, retrieved March 15, 2023, https://www.mckinsey.com/industries/healthcare/our-insights/overcoming-stigma-three-strategies-toward-better-mental-health-in-the-workplace.

to perpetuate this narrative in the so-called 'evolved' era we live in today.

An emotionally inclusive workplace tackles stigma as its top priority. It offers perspective and awareness on what stigma means and the distress it causes individuals. There is no question that emotionally inclusive companies communicate tools and strategies to address and spot anxiety, depression, stress, and mental illness overall. Some examples of such measures include regular check-ins with the company's in-house psychologist, educational programmes, self-assessment tests, and the like. They remove shame from mental health by openly addressing the relevance of it in the workplace today. Such companies will, for example, work to expose the implicit and explicit biases. Bosses can think of themselves as being non-judgmental, but when a subordinate opens about their suicidal thoughts or their recent bipolar diagnosis, they may instinctively make a host of false assumptions or fall into the judgement trap. To shed light on our own levels of unconscious bias, tools such as the Implicit Association Test can be used to measure workplace partialities *(for lack of really wanting to say 'prejudices')* and stereotypes. It could also aid companies in achieving a better understanding and greater awareness of the beliefs and attitudes employees are unable to report, because of their implicit nature.

Going back to mental health stigma at work, it is also worth noting that stigma directly impacts how we choose to express ourselves. The reality is that not all displays of emotions are treated equally. For example, happy but personal news of a colleague's engagement is likely to be received well, while people may react hesitantly on hearing about a colleague's revelation of issues such as depression. This is so enmeshed into our unspoken workplace norms that few have the awareness to pick up on this. In a piece for BBC, journalist Zulekha Nathoo writes that 'what is and isn't considered "appropriate" can depend on the worker'[56]. This means, for example, that women who cry at work are assumed to be unprofessional, while men doing the same are given the benefit of the doubt, as people assume they are dealing with external factors[57].

Challenging Stigma

My greatest wish for the world is to witness an Emotional inclusion sea change in the workplace. The stigmatized conventional thinking that is suggested today in the arena of mental health or Emotional wellness is the direct consequence of a culture that has been on autopilot, a culture that is flawed through its failure to address core Emotional humanitarian needs.

The stigma surrounding mental health is still so prevalent *because* it is still negatively correlated to mental illness. All this does is 'lead individuals to be discredited by society and experience barriers surrounding employment, access to care, and social support'[58]. As Michelle Obama points out, 'Getting support and treatment isn't a sign of weakness, it's a sign of strength'.[59] *It sure is.* An employee battling depression, an anxiety disorder, bipolar disorder, ADHD, schizophrenia, an eating disorder, or any other

---

[56] Nathoo, Z. (2021, October 29) 'The people penalised for expressing feelings at work', *BBC*, retrieved February 27, 2023, https://www.bbc.com/worklife/article/20211029-the-people-penalised-for-expressing-feelings-at-work.

[57] Elsbach, K.D., & Bechky, B.A. (2018, June 25), 'How Observers Assess Women Who Cry in Professional Work Contexts', Academy of Management Discoveries, 4(2)' https://doi.org/10.5465/amd.2016.0025.

[58] Bharadwaj, P., Pai, M.M., & Suziedelyte, A. (2017, July), 'Emotional wellness Stigma', *Economics Letters*, 159, 53–56. 10.1016/j.econlet.2017.06.028.

[59] Obama, M. (2015, March 4), 'Remarks by The First lady at "Change Direction" Emotional wellness event', retrieved February 22, 2023, from https://obamawhitehouse.archives.gov/the-press-office/2015/03/04/remarks-first-lady-change-direction-mental-health-event.

mental health disorder must be able to feel safe to speak up about it openly. *Catalysing fear around stigma is what drives people to their graves.*

With mental illness comes deep human suffering. It is oftentimes a lonely journey which is made even lonelier when having to put up a front and not show an ounce of emotion. Researchers at the Institute of Psychiatry at King's College London examined data from 144 studies, which included over 90,000 participants worldwide. Do you know what they found? They found that the stigma of mental illness is one of the *top* reasons that people do not receive care[60]. This invariably has profound negative effects on how one shows up in the world, and, surely enough, how one shows up at work. In my organization, Emotional inclusion® In The Workplace, I call on CEOs, global leaders, and movers and shakers to shift their moral obligation to stop the stigmatization of mental health and to stop waterproofing the subject matter. The stakes are simply too high.

Harbouring emotionally inclusive spaces in our workplace breeds 'psychological safety'—a concept universalized by Dr Amy C Edmondson that we discussed in an earlier chapter—which leads, she reasons, to candour[61] and a greater sense of belonging. Exercising humility, vulnerability, and curiosity makes for a powerful triage, she explains, and I could not agree with her more. When we share our struggles within this backdrop, psychological safety is harboured, and authentic human connection is made possible.

---

[60] Clement, S., Schauman, O., Graham, T., Maggioni, F., Evans-Lack, S., Bezborodovs, N., Morgan, C., Rüsch, N., Brown, J.S.L., & Thornicroft, G. (2015, January) 'What is the impact of Emotional wellness-related stigma on help-seeking? A systematic review of quantitative and qualitative studies', *Psychological Medicine*, 45(1), 11–27. 10.1017/S0033291714000129.

[61] Episode 20 Ei x Amy Edmondson: 'When Psychological Safety & Emotional inclusion Come Together', *Emotional Inclusion*, retrieved February 22, 2023, https://www.emotionalinclusion.com/podcast-amy-edmondson/.

You might now be wondering how to challenge workplace stigma. It is a fair question to ask. There are, of course, the avenues I have already mentioned to explore, but at the most basic level, everyone, particularly leaders, can begin by educating themselves more on the topic of mental illnesses. Then we have specific evidence-based strategies that are found to reduce stigma, released by the National Academy of Sciences, Engineering, and Medicine[62]. These include:

- Education, such as mental health literacy campaigns
- Protest and advocacy (e.g., letter writing and Twitter campaigns)
- Programmes that facilitate social contact between people with and without behavioural disorders (contact-based programs)
- Contact-based education programmes, which combine contact with educational content designed to raise public awareness of selected issues or increase public knowledge about mental and substance use disorders
- Media campaigns delivered over a range of platforms, including traditional and newer social media
- Peer programmes in which people who have disclosed their conditions offer their experience and expertise to individuals and families, ranging from informal peer-led programmes to peer-specialized services in health services systems

As people become more aware of its impacts, mental health at large will slowly become more understood and recognized

---

[62] Nieweglowski, K., & Sheehan, L. (2017) 'The National Academy of Sciences releases report on the stigma of behavioral health', *Stigma and Health*, 2(3), 157–158, APA PsychNet, retrieved February 22, 2023, https://psycnet.apa.org/doiLanding?doi=10.1037%2Fsah0000094.

among the general population. It is a process that will not happen in a vacuum, even though I wish it did.

In the meantime, award-winning mental health writer Natasha Tracy recommends focusing on obtaining treatment over battling stigma. 'It can be difficult if people around you can't accept your mental illness treatment but, first and foremost, treatment is about getting you better and bringing people onside is a secondary concern', she said in an interview[63]. Indeed, awareness of mental health issues is still meagre. Compared to the pink ribbon, which has been used to raise awareness of breast cancer, few are familiar with the green ribbon, which is used to represent mental health awareness. I orchestrated a 'mental health unfiltered' event last year with two leading psychologists and two mental health advocates (of which I was one) and congregated a room full of C-suites, press, and mental health business drivers. Each guest was given a green ribbon, but most had no knowledge about its significance—a telling sign that the taboo around discussing mental health is still too much for most.

Fighting stigma against mental health or Emotional wellness will take continued awareness efforts to promote understanding and acceptance for tangible change to occur. There is no bypassing the fact that perpetuating long-term change calls for widespread interventions, and companies have the moral obligation (which I am purposefully repeating here) to take action on this and spearhead greater impact.

Why? People bury their struggles and stories under the pressure to avoid stigma altogether, as widespread reluctance to address mental health still lingers in the workplace and discourages employees from speaking up. Yet this falsely signals to employers

---

[63] Krans, B. (2018, October 20), 'Stigma Still a Major Hurdle in Getting People the Mental Health Care They Need', *Healthline*, retrieved February 22, 2023, https://www.healthline.com/health-news/mental-health-treatment-hindered-by-stigma-030214#Some-Advice-From-a-Stigma-Breaker.

that mental health is, by definition, not a pressing issue. False assessments are still overwhelmingly common in the workplace, and we must collectively and actively change the script. When did we stop being gentle to ourselves and to others? Deadening our emotions at the office and numbing ourselves with food, sex, drugs, or sheer denial only prevents us from looking at exactly what needs healing, softness, and compassion. If you ask me, this not the true path of the corporate Emotional wellness warrior.

Employers are starting to understand the gravity of the problem and are slowly opening up to the concept of Emotional wellness at work. So too are employees, and discussion of mental health challenges has become more commonplace in the office[64]. In the UK, a third of workers now feel more comfortable talking about their workplace mental health, compared to before the pandemic[65]. It is a similar story in the US: the number of workers comfortable talking openly about mental health with their supervisors jumped from five in ten in 2019 to six in ten in 2020[66].

In the aftermath of the pandemic, we are seeing how stories of mental health stigma are starting to emerge. I will share some with you—from friends, fellow colleagues, and global leaders—in a subsequent chapter. The voices behind these stories call us to

---

[64] Carnegie, M. (2022, August 24) 'Is workplace stigma around mental health struggles changing?' BBC, retrieved February 23, 2023, from https://www. bbc.com/worklife/article/20220819-is-workplace-stigma-around-mental-health-struggles-changing.

[65] 'My Whole Self Day 2022', MHFA England, (2022, March 17), retrieved February 23, 2023, from https://mhfaengland.org/mhfa-centre/news/my-whole-self-day-2022/.

[66] 'New APA Poll Shows Surge in Anxiety Among Americans Top Causes Are Safety, COVID-19, Health, Gun Violence, and the Upcoming Election', American Psychiatric Association, (2020, October 21), retrieved February 23, 2023, https://www.psychiatry.org/newsroom/news-releases/anxiety-poll-2020.

openly have a conversation and authentically communicate around the subject matter of Emotional inclusion. They also call out the unfortunate gap in overall education and understanding around the subject matter. These stories depict how much more work there is to be done in changing our mindset about Emotional inclusivity in and around mental health or Emotional wellness. Yet a glimmer of hope emerges as I notice that an awakening of sorts is now surfacing within the pool of mass consciousness—that people simply do not want to put up with inhuman workplaces anymore and they are now starting to speak up.

This is, in turn, moving the needle and companies are beginning to offer various types of support such as extra paid time off, mental health days (which is a tricky one because not everyone feels 'comfortable' taking them), mental health or Emotional wellness training for executives and staff, etc. Yet the disconnect between experiencing mental health challenges and continuing having to perform at work still clash. And unless we are relentless in creating grassroots structures to accommodate the said issue, no advancements will be made.

This will take work, since change needs to happen at the top, says Naeema Pasha, EMEA director of behavioural science at digital coaching platform CoachHub[67]. She adds, 'All the constituent parts of workplace well-being, destigmatization included, must be integrated at an executive-strategy level, and be a collective priority, not one that sits purely with HR teams'. Let us see what our global leaders have to say about this in the next chapter, but I would like to close this one with an insightful story.

---

[67] Carnegie, M. (2022, August 24) 'Is workplace stigma around mental health struggles changing?' BBC, retrieved February 26, 2023, https://www.bbc.com/worklife/article/20220819-is-workplace-stigma-around-mental-health-struggles-changing.

When I interviewed former Southeast Asia President of Johnson & Johnson (J&J), Jan Meurer, on my Emotional inclusion podcast, he spoke about the company credo, written by Robert Wood Johnson, former chairman and member of the founding family of J&J, who presided over the conglomerate from 1932 to 1963. Robert crafted the credo in 1943 during the 'hot' phase of the Industrial Revolution, right before the company became a publicly traded one, so that it would not lose the value system of its founding days. He championed a stigma-free workplace well before anyone else did, and there was no question that it was revolutionary at the time.

To quote the second paragraph of the credo, Robert enforced that 'we are responsible for our employees who work for us throughout the world. We must provide an inclusive work environment where each person must be considered as an individual. We must respect their diversity and dignity and recognize their merit. They must have a sense of security, fulfilment and purpose in their jobs. Compensation must be fair and adequate and working conditions clean, orderly and safe. We must support the health and wellbeing of our employees and help them fulfil their family and other personal responsibilities. Employees must feel free to make suggestions and complaint. There must be equal opportunity for employment, development and advancement for those qualified. We must provide highly capable leaders and their actions must be just and ethical'.[68] This now-eighty-year-old credo, so deeply vested in J&J's success, could not hold more relevance than it does today within the context of Emotional inclusion. As Jan puts it, this remarkable

---

[68] Meurer, Jan (2020, July 3) 'Emotional Inclusion at Johnson &Johnson', Emotional Inclusion Podcast, https://podcasts.apple.com/ph/podcast/ei-johnson-johnson/id1518433002?i=1000482231083.

document shows the responsibility of the corporation to its employees and has guided the company through every crisis to become one of the top ten most valuable companies in the world today[69]. Jan went on to say that this segment of the credo 'almost contains all ideas of what Emotional inclusion is ultimately about. It is about individuals, it is about dignity, it is about recognizing their merit, it is about equal opportunity, it is about taking care of the working conditions of our employees'. Whenever the company encounters a difficult situation, they take out the document and read it again. And then it drives their decisions, enabling them to do the right thing.

---

[69] Mora, Carolina Car (2023, April 7) 'What are the Top 10 Most Valuable Companies in the World 2023?' Admiral Markets, https://admiralmarkets. com/education/articles/shares/most-valuable-companies.

Key Takeaways

- Even today, showing emotion at the workplace is not 'safe'. It has been stigmatized and opens us up to judgment, negative labels, and dismissal. Stigma acts as a barrier to Emotional inclusion; it results in people working to appear upbeat and positive at all times in the office, even as they grapple with suffering.

- The stigma surrounding mental health is widely prevalent because it is still negatively correlated to mental illness. This is also one of the top reasons why people suffering from mental health issues do not receive care; they bury their struggles under the pressure to avoid stigma. And because employees do not speak up, this falsely signals to employers that mental health is not a pressing issue.

- We need a movement around mental health or Emotional wellness in the workplace, where organizations seek to develop emotionally inclusive spaces that foster 'psychological safety' and lead to candour. When we are vulnerable with others, we are open to more meaningful and real discussions that build valuable human connections in a company. Compassion in the midst of pain and fear should be the way of the corporate mental health or Emotional wellness warrior.

- To bring about such change, everyone, particularly leaders, can begin by educating themselves on the topic of mental illnesses, and thereafter pursuing more avenues of mental health support, such as advocacy, storytelling, social media campaigns, and programmes that increase awareness of mental illness or that facilitate connection with persons with mental health issues.

- Fighting stigma against mental health will take continued effort. There is no bypassing the fact that long-term change calls for widespread intervention, and as organizations with power over the work lives of hundreds, if not thousands, of people, companies have the moral obligation to spearhead these efforts.

- Cultivating an environment of trust involves acknowledging that emotions are an integral part of our biology that enable us to pilot our way through life. Being able to 'not be okay' should no longer be viewed as a sign of unprofessionalism. An employee battling depression, anxiety, ADHD, or any other mental health disorder should be able to feel safe to speak up about it openly. This change in perception will take time, but the benefits far outweigh the drawbacks.

- In the aftermath of the pandemic, employers are starting to understand the gravity of the problem and are slowly opening up to the concept of mental health or Emotional wellness at work. So too are employees. We are seeing how stories of Emotional wellness start to emerge from workplaces, and this could be a promising sign that change is coming.

Part IV

What Global Leaders Have to Say

'People talk about the digital revolution, but I think the Emotional inclusion revolution has taken a big step forward.'[70]

—ALAIN LI (former RICHEMONT CEO, Asia Pacific)

As a leader myself, I have lived in Africa, France, and America. And for the past seventeen years, I have resided in Hong Kong, and now Singapore, where I work as General Manager for Longchamp (Singapore and Malaysia), a French luxury leather goods company. I am often asked what has kept me so long in the same company, to which I always swiftly respond 'the humanistic leadership'. Longchamp is one of the few family-owned fashion companies today that has not been snatched up by a huge conglomerate; and I have the utmost respect for its owners. The

---

[70] Li, Alain (2021, Feb 24) 'Emotional Inclusion x Richemont With Alain Li', *Emotional Inclusion Podcast*, https://podcasts.apple.com/ph/podcast/emotional-inclusion-x-richemont-with-alain-li/id1518433002?i=1000510394141.

third-generation President, Jean Cassegrain, is someone I deeply respect and admire. His ability to lead with humility, curiosity, and genuine care for his employees have always really touched me. How we comport ourselves as leaders, how we choose to treat other people does not need to fit under the heavy blanket of old-fashioned ways. Jean and his entire family are living proof of that, and they have been such an inspiration to me.

Being a good leader is about defending those who cannot defend themselves. It is only sensible that we view strong ethical, inclusive leadership as a by-product of Emotional inclusion. In times of upheaval, leaders have the lion's share of responsibility to be the change in order to drive organizational success. All the inspired leaders whom I esteem and whom I have had the privilege to meet or work with think from the inside out. I have spent a long time during my professional career observing what makes great leaders great. The common denominators I have found are their ability to:

- Be brave enough to be vulnerable
- Put their egos to the side to leave centre stage to humility
- Exercise curiosity and empathy
- Execute clear vision of what they want to achieve whilst being open to new ideas
- Make time for others even when they are 'time-starved'
- Give back to society through valuable contribution, for the greater good.

Simply put, good leaders—those who are makers of change—navigate through the school of life by drawing and exemplifying the very best of it. They have all tasted the meaning of pain, grief, and loss. And yet it has not barraged their ethical, human sensical leadership ethos. I agree with Swiss-American psychiatrist Elisabeth Kübler-Ross when she writes that 'the most beautiful people we have known are those who have known defeat, known suffering, known struggle, known loss, and have found their way out of the depths'.[71]

Such people, Kübler-Ross writes, understand that 'beautiful people do not just happen', instead, they have 'an appreciation, a sensitivity, and an understanding of life that fills them with compassion, gentleness, and a deep loving concern'. And so, to me, to be a 'beautiful leader' calls on us to be kind with our people, to care for their well-being, to always bear in mind that life exists beyond simply the demands of the workplaces, in areas much closer to the heart, like health, family, and love.

What Makes a Good Leader?

Nothing in life that is worth doing is ever easy. Yet leaders are morally responsible to use their voice, boldly and bravely, with the knowledge that there can be no progress without struggle. The leaders who do *make a difference* stand out from the pack. They know how to utilize, through innate steering of their intuition, both their intellect and their emotions. At the intersection of this, and key to the concept of exercising Emotional inclusion as a leader is intellectual humility. It is a willingness to reconsider views, to not always be 'right', and to respond to being challenged without being defensive. It is the ability to take in new evidence when informing views, to be less concerned about self-importance, and to resist the natural urge to strongly prioritize one's own needs[72].

'Humility', the theologian and philosopher St Augustine famously wrote, 'is the foundation of all other virtues'[73]. And we need humility in order to accept that we all have different reactions

---

[71] Kübler-Ross, E. (1975) *Death: The Final Stage of Growth*, Prentice-Hall.

[72] 'Intellectual Humility', John Templeton Foundation, retrieved February 23, 2023, https://www.templeton.org/discoveries/intellectual-humility/.

[73] Augustine, as cited in (2016) *Cultivating Virtue: Self-Mastery with the Saints*, TAN Books, https://tanbooks.com/products/books/spiritual-warfare/virtue-vice/cultivating-virtue-self-mastery-with-the-saints/.

to life. Humility is a form of reverence and respect to the other. Dr Amy C Edmondson furthers the discussion by framing the fact that curiosity is the twin sister of humility and empathy[74].

So, if you were to ask how do we measure the humility of an individual, I would say, well, do not ask the leaders who are intellectually humble, ask the people who know them. When you examine the lives of the most influential captains of industry, you discover commonalities that are indisputably evident.

In my opinion, these are:

- Humility
- Alignment with their purpose
- Curiosity
- Kindness (giving their time when they are starved of it)
- Empathy

There are, of course, many more attributes that make up a good leader, however these top five specifically are the are traits I very much attribute to emotionally inclusive leaders.

Why so? Well for one, their strong moral codes mean they tend to focus on creating a fair and inclusive environment for all. For another, their focus on communication positions them well to listen to the stories of others and, in turn, to share their own. Third, leaders with this combination of traits tend to place positive psychology at the heart of their leadership and are most likely to find Emotional inclusion an important and urgent priority.

The origin of the word 'lead' in Old English is *lædan* (transitive), meaning 'to guide'. Weak leaders are the ones that do not take care of their people, do not listen to their needs, and do not provide

---

[74] 'Episode 20 Ei x Amy Edmondson: "When Psychological Safety & Emotional inclusion Come Together"', *Emotional Inclusion*, retrieved February 22, 2023, https://www.emotionalinclusion.com/podcast-amy-edmondson/.

the guidance needed to navigate mental wellness at work. They perpetuate archaic ways of work—like a KPI-driven culture, or a vicious system where staff who speak up about their emotions are penalized in terms of performance, put under greater scrutiny, or pushed out of their jobs. These bosses prioritize productivity and profit over welfare and well-being and continue to not allocate sufficient—or, in cases, any—budget for mental health. It is an indirect way of telling workers that they do not care. And there is not a doubt in my mind that these leaders, who do not advocate for the wellness of their people, will inevitably, one way or the other, pay the price at an organizational bottom line. It is life-changing and it is life-saving in so many ways to have that one person (notably your boss) listen to you with compassion and respond to your mental health or Emotional wellness needs. We simply cannot call ourselves emotionally inclusive if we do not play our part on a humanistic leadership front.

This is why I dedicated this chapter to what global leaders have to say. In the next section, I will share with you the personal journeys of leaders who live by the principles of Emotional inclusion. These are leaders who have known and confronted suffering, and who have moulded their experience into driving change for good within the arena of Emotional inclusion. Being emotionally inclusive is about speaking up boldly and bravely about our humanness in the workplace and tackling it in a laser-focused way, come hell or high water. And it is no easy feat to perform. It takes courage, it takes determination, it takes grit, it takes purpose, and it takes a whole lot of drive. I am proud to feature these Emotional inclusion 'compatriots' because I know, all too well, how it feels.

It would be disingenuous of me to talk about Emotional inclusion, to include real life stories from my fellow peers, and not speak of my own journey. Emotional inclusion also means choosing to walk the path of courage and doing so with vulnerability and honesty. Putting aside fear and shame while accepting our own humanness. As Brené Brown puts it so well, 'Vulnerability sounds like truth and feels like courage. Truth and courage aren't always comfortable, but they're never weakness'.[75] I know this concept to be true, while our society, on the other hand, is still failingly struggling with it.

The truth is that we are all more same than we are different. We are so ashamed of our emotions that we minimize them out of fear. I was once reminded that bravery in the face of fear is called courage. And courage is, well, 'courage is fear walking'.[76] I just adore this line by Susan David, a global authority in the realm of Emotional agility. As we voyage through the peaks and the valleys of our lives, let us please do each other the ultimate favour of all: let us please be unapologetically human with each other. It is oftentimes easier said than done, I realize, but let us give it a good hard try, shall we?

[75] Brown, B. (2012) *Daring Greatly*, Penguin Publishing Group.

[76] David, S. (2022, May 6) 'Courage in the Face of Fear', Susan David, retrieved February 23, 2023, https://www.susandavid.com/newsletter/courage-in-the-face-of-fear/.

Stories of Emotional inclusion

Olivier Krueger, Global CEO, Lufthansa Systems

When Mollie asked me to join her movement for Emotional inclusion, right away two stories came to my mind which today are somewhat implemented in our company and certainly in my understanding of modern leadership.

My father—who was a high-ranking diplomat with a PhD in Law, who speaks more than sixteen languages—made it very clear to us three children: 'Work hard, and have a plan on what you want to be in the future', insinuating that we should become a lawyer, a doctor, a teacher, or anything equally recognized in society.

In other words, he (strictly) encouraged us to connect the dots through a specific plan without asking us what WE really wanted to be. And much later, I found out the hard way that this was HIS idea of my life, but not mine.

Consequently, I studied law, my sister studied medicine, and guess what, my brother embarked on becoming a teacher. Very quickly I found out that my passion was not to become a lawyer. However, since I 'knew' I had to 'just' work hard to connect the dots, I continued for quite a while. I started feeling miserable and got sick without understanding that these two things were connected.

Even though I was a strong young man, I found myself again and again at the doctor's, until one doctor sent me to seek psychological support. I was irritated, felt misunderstood, and certainly would neither tell my father nor anyone else. After all, everyone was full of expectations of me being the next great lawyer in the family.

Today it is common knowledge that wrong pressure eventually leads to illness and the need for help to repair what went wrong in the first place. The psychological support—at that time something to be kept secret— plus the valuable advice of the partner's wife in the law firm I worked at eventually changed my life more than anything else.

Both the therapy and the advice helped me to start steering my own life again. They looked at my passions, my inner compass, my interests, my genuine idea of life. They taught me to create circumstances that would later, in retrospect, beautifully connect the dots. I failed my law exams shortly after and changed my life drastically. I started studying international relations and later obtained a master's in political science & sociology from one of the 'Grande écoles' in France.

I became an outstanding student, started listening to my inner compass, and my body. I started doing sports, got myself engaged in topics I was really interested in and did not care about what others expected from me, in the best possible sense. Suddenly, I didn't find myself at the doctor's anymore and I wasn't tired in the morning. Work became a pleasure I could not get enough of. I had learned that psychological well-being, safety, and stability were equally important as physical health.

So how does this affect my leadership style today and what were we able to learn as an organization? First, I deeply understood that, as a leader, I do have a significant influence on the psychological safety of my direct reports and, thus, on our whole organization. Today the Lufthansa Group carefully selects its managers all the way up to top management applying Leadership-Next-Level principles, including psychological safety. In addition, we have therapists in our group who work anonymously to provide support.

With my own story in mind, I aim to create an environment which allows our employees to find out—if they have not already—what their real passion is and then to support them on their path. This starts right at the beginning during the hiring process.

In former times, one had to apply for a job in our company, and we as a corporation decided whether we wanted to give the applicant the opportunity to fulfil a role we had designed to our needs only. Today our hiring process is fundamentally different. E.g., when applying for a role as personal assistant, we do not have a clear role description. We invite candidates for a talk on eye level. We apply to be an employer as much as the candidate applies for a job, which is designed around the passion and capabilities of the candidate. Thus, we only outline general areas but not specific duties, with the exception of pilots, medical staff, etc., though the eye level principle still applies.

I believe there is no difference between a broken arm and a psychological imbalance caused by Emotional exclusion—both need to be cured. Yes, it is a lot more effort to take that path, but I strongly believe that this leads to healthier employees on a holistic level. And reality shows we are on the right track!

Lyn Lee, Vice President, Diversity, Equity, and Inclusion, Shell, Asia

'Do I look like a failure to you?' That was the question I asked a group of youth leaders at an event a few years back where I was invited to speak about my experience with mood disorder. They said no. I asked them this to show them that having a mental illness need not stop one from being successful and achieving goals in life. Prior to being diagnosed, I had not known that mood disorders, if left unmanaged, can lead to extreme mood swings of Emotional highs (hyper mania) and lows (depression). But these emotions do not define me. They are products of the condition, which I have since learnt to manage.

Life stressors can bring about mental health issues. It was the perfect storm for me. I had lost my father to cancer and was also going through a divorce after being married for eighteen years. I was also travelling a lot for work. This added tremendous pressure on me. When the symptoms started to emerge, it was gradual. I started feeling tired, was not able to have sound sleep, had less motivation to do things which I loved, and I was distracted and not able to focus, and I was a Global HR manager at Shell at that point. I did not miss a day of work because I loved my job, but I was struggling. Eventually, it came to a point where I just could not get out of bed.

My sister urged me to see a psychiatrist, and I am glad she did. She did not judge; she simply acknowledged that I was not okay and told me I would be okay again with some help. That is what we all need when we are struggling with our mental well-being—a strong social support system and empathy, as opposed to sympathy. I would not have known I have a mental health issue had I not sought medical attention. Most of us tend to dismiss the symptoms or attribute it to stress or even hormones when it is a woman. We think we can just shake it off, but we cannot just snap out of depression—it is a medical condition.

With the diagnosis, I felt a veil was lifted. I cannot quite describe it, but I felt relieved and, with that, had instant clarity. Seeing a psychiatrist helped me but I always highlight that recovery takes time, so do not be discouraged if it feels like things do not get better immediately.

I had a close working relationship with my leader, and I did not hesitate to inform him of my condition. He was kind and compassionate and asked me what I needed to manage my workload so I could take care of myself. I am one of the lucky ones. Being brought up in a supportive family enabled me to feel it was all right to tell my boss. It also helped that there is a culture of respect and inclusion at Shell. My leaders supported me in taking the time I needed to recover, and they meant what they said. I did not have the barrier many persons struggling with Emotional unwellness face. Emotional unwellness continues to be stigmatized. Many worry they will be penalized, or that they will not have a job to come back to if they have to take time out from work. These issues are the realities of struggling with Emotional unwellness and the double whammy of not being as productive or not performing at work.

We have to make empathy the norm. Creating an inclusive work culture and supporting those with mental health issues are not just about ticking the boxes. It is the right thing to do. For me, success in this area means making a positive impact on employees' lived experience. It means making self-care and building resilience a top priority in the organization. It is about leaders role-modelling empathy and care and building trust with their teams to build Emotional capital. It means providing training for employees to be allies and ambassadors, so that they can spot the first signs of someone needing help. It takes a mindset of inclusion and for leaders to approach with heart and kindness and implement policies with employees' well-being in mind. Organizations should come on board to address mental health issues and be a force that promotes change. In the end, the employees' lived experience is the true measure of how far and successful an organization has come in destigmatizing Emotional unwellness in the organization. Employees should be able to bring their whole selves to work.

It is OK to not be OK. When we talk about making the workplace inclusive, the discussion should also involve making it safe—both physically and psychologically. To stress this, we rolled out a campaign at Shell called 'I'm not OK' to destigmatize mental illness and create a workplace where it is okay to reach out and say 'I'm not OK.' We want to be there for our staff who need support and help because, ultimately, we can only perform at our best when we are well.

I still see my psychiatrist once every six months. These reviews are important, just as how we see the doctor for our blood pressure or sugar level if we are diabetic. These sessions give me a full-picture awareness of my condition and help me to manage it effectively. So, when I am at my low and do not feel like doing anything, I make sure I keep active. Physical exercise has become an important part of my routine.

And at my high, I remind myself to slow down, breathe, pause, and be calm. Over the years, practising mindfulness has also helped me to manage myself. This comes with an appreciation of what the illness is. I advocate being physically active whether or not you have a mental health condition. But especially for people with mental health issues, exercising is a great way to release positive hormones and manage stress. I go to the gym three to four times a week, and I also practise gyrotonic, a training method based on the principles of yoga and dance. It builds core strength, balance, coordination, and agility, thus benefiting both my physical and mental well-being. In recent years, I have practised taking more time out for myself and pursue my love for trekking and being in nature.

Find your purpose and meaning. Find your bigger purpose and pursue things which give you meaning and joy. Most of us want to lead a meaningful life. I feel called to do work, in my professional role, which impacts under-represented communities. For someone who has experienced what it is *like to suffer from Emotional unwellness, that is the silver lining—you can actually do good by spreading this awareness. But you cannot do this effectively unless you take care of yourself first. Seek help, and then make sure that you surround yourself with people who can provide support and make you feel safe, physically and psychologically.*

Gordon Watson, CEO, AXA, Asia and Africa

I grew up in Glasgow in a more chichi part of town, however, every day I saw people being bullied for no reason. If you were slightly effeminate, lived in a large house, or had a slightly different accent, you were game for abuse. In fact, there was no real reason other than the mood of the 'stronger' and more 'in' kids.

I watched as people were physically and mentally abused. I tried my best to stop this where I could, but looking back and on reflection, I am ashamed I did not do a whole lot more. I was not bullied much, as I sort of fit into a 'norm' of being decent at sports and had nothing too obvious to be picked on for—however, there was one kid who for some reason did not like the way I looked. I had some inbuilt protection, as I had many stronger friends from the football team who could take my side as needed, but even given that, I was still very affected by this mental torment. I can remember every small incident even to this day.

The one thing I hold dear is fairness and an inclusive culture. I reflect I had an easier upbringing, but even this one guy made me feel threatened every day at school. As I compare my experience with those around me, I question how they must have felt and that must have been truly unthinkable. While many of those people who had this experience are living all over the world now and thriving in places where they can be themselves, others are not so lucky. It is not just Glasgow, it is everywhere.

I was recently interviewed by Todd Sears from OutLeadership and he asked me why a CEO with a shaved head who loves football is such an advocate for his community. I had to really think about this. I recalled the real turning point of realization as a young adult was when I listened to a song called 'Small Town Boy' by Bronski Beat. It is a song about leaving town after being bullied. I have goosebumps when I hear this song. These lyrics can apply to anyone and everyone, even the bullied or even more so, the bullies, as they are the ones with many more insecurities.

Inclusiveness and promoting mental health have become a mission for me. It was not a choice I made. One day, it just happened. I had a close friend take his own life; I had no idea what he was going through. I was helping him find a job and found him a few contacts and was rather surprised and upset when he said those roles were above him. They certainly were not. I just thought he was modest; I saw no warning signs.

I started to write about mental health on LinkedIn. I had many people privately contact me to share their experiences confidentially. I was taken aback as the people who approached me were not people I would ever have guessed were struggling. It was invisible, and they made sure it was invisible. The stigma was too much for them to out themselves as having mental health problems.

I felt like a bit of a fraud as I had people talking to me about their innermost feelings and struggles, but I had no training in what to say to them. I decided to pursue a master's degree in global mental health (fittingly at the university of Glasgow, the same town I grew up and got bullied in) to understand more. At the time of writing, I have just completed my final dissertation and hope to graduate soon. I realized I could use my role to help business leaders understand the best practices to support those in the workforce who are struggling, and also provide more upstream preventative programmes.

I often wonder who made me want to do this more: the person who bullied me, or the people I saw who were never given a chance. I feel, and hope, this work will make a difference to mental health in the workplace. My personal mantra is 'I am the king of my now' and while I cannot go back and have a 'do over' of what happened at school, I can at least do this now at this point in my life to make a bit of a difference.

I became the Chair of the founding member companies of a tripartite venture for OneMind (a US-based mental health NGO), Columbia University, and Ethisphere in launching a 'Mental Health at Work' index that will help business leaders measure the maturity of their mental health culture and benchmark it against evidence-based best practices. My research found that this type of help for business leaders was lacking. The index will also have the capability to provide advice on areas where company programmes are weak, with recommendations on what they have to do to improve, based on guidelines by the World Health Organization and more.

I believe in the importance of Emotional inclusion as it calls for humanity in a way that puts Emotional wellbeing at the very centre of business agendas and creates true shared value.

Maya Hari, *Climate Tech CEO at Terrascope, TEDx Speaker, Ex Vice President at Twitter*

There was a time when I worked for a global tech and digital darling of a company, which has long been lauded as an amazing place to work as a marketing leader in Asia. I had vowed to stay committed to the role I passionately inhabited despite being seven months pregnant at the time. Every marketing campaign would have to be reviewed by a global team before being approved for launch. The global team, full of wonderful, kind, and creative souls, were also mindful of their commitment to their families and only worked within a set working hours in the US. This meant that I was presenting a marketing campaign to this team (who I genuinely liked as individuals) at 3 a.m. my time.

My partner and I talked about this, and I wondered if I had my priorities right in life, whether I was endangering my unborn daughter's well-being by doing this meeting at an insane hour.

In retrospect the discussion should never have been about my priorities in life. It should have been about whether the company was setting up processes to be inclusive to all its employees around the world. How should the company help teams build Emotional inclusion to include all employees?

I realized later, as I worked in a different global social and digital company, that building an emotionally inclusive culture is both a science and an art worth mastering. Working tirelessly to think about nuanced ways to make someone feel like they belong in the company, in the office, in their team, is the most critical pursuit in building an amazing culture.

Mollie Jean De Dieu, General Manager, Longchamp, Singapore and Malaysia, Founder of Emotional Inclusion® in the Workforce

We have all experienced our fair share of hardships; mine are no more special or unique than anyone else's. I am oftentimes asked why I felt called to deputize Emotional inclusion in the workforce, and clearly, besides the countless stories I have witnessed and been privy to, my own battles have also very evidently fuelled my belief that no one can properly function at work when experiencing adversities. Our home-selves and our work-selves are one, we simply cannot split ourselves in half for the sake of appearing 'normal', put together, and shieldless in the school of life.

In my two-decade long corporate career, I, too, have lived through my own rollercoaster of struggles. From losing a child to going through the hardest hurdle I have ever experienced in my life right at this very moment. A divorce.

One breath at a time, I am experiencing eleven years of marriage trickle down the drain. Divorce, for those of you who have not gone through it, is brutally difficult. A punch in the gut, a day-to-day journey of walking the hard miles of grief, letting go, and forgiveness. A breaking of a family unit that will never operate the same together, ever again. A chapter of life closed forever, when there was never meant to be an end to it.

I pondered long and hard as to sharing my story as it is all so very raw and so distressingly current. Yet if we are going to be transparently honest with each other in shedding light on our own humanity for the

sake of making Emotional inclusion the new status quo, then making myself vulnerable to you and to the world is exactly where it all begins. Vulnerability is truly the gateway to authentic human connection.

Truth be told, I have always been really good at hiding my emotions at work and keeping my pain nicely tucked away. Portraying the woman who could handle it all whilst secretly rolling with the punches of life was me performing under the societal and workplace expectations we are all so well-versed with and yet keeping so quiet about the unspoken stigma behind not being at the top of one's game, day in and day out, looms large. If it were not, well, clearly this book on Emotional inclusion would not be worth seeing the light of day.

When I finally broke the news to my boss about my divorce, he was surprised and confessed that he would never have guessed. In hindsight, it is not something I feel proud of, especially amidst all the advocacy work I do around Emotional inclusion. Yet I am cognizant of the fact that we all have our own coping mechanisms and that there is a time for everything in life: a time to take a breath and digest our hardships, a time to speak up on them, and finally, a time to act upon them for the better. As I became more open and vocal about my divorce at work, I was received with a lot of compassion and genuine care. Amidst the fact that there are no Emotional well-being platforms instilled in the organization just yet (a work in progress as they are on their way), the 'how are you's became more meaningful.

Whilst I am and have always been a passionate supporter of therapy and have been seeing a therapist outside the realm of work for many years now, I was having trouble multitasking as easily as I used to. I felt extremely exhausted, mentally and physically. Truth be told, it is still all a glorious juggle at times. Promoting Emotional inclusion and acting upon it in our workplaces today does not make me a mental health or Emotional wellness superstar. I am a human being, just like you are.

My marriage was meant for a season. I have made peace with that, and if I were asked if I would do it all over again, my answer would be yes. Yes, I would, because the very foundations of what I have lived through have led me to where I am today. To a place where I know first-hand how much Emotional inclusion is needed in our world and how much the workplace, particularly, is starved of it. It further catalysed my belief for the need of internalized, medicalized, and confidential aid in our organizations. And I will continue to champion this with unwavering dedication.

If I may, the stigma attached to Emotional unwellness is well above and beyond outdated. I do not know of one single human being who has not known pain. I find that looking at it this way can help in expanding our awareness of how we choose to navigate our struggles and as a consequence, how we choose to treat each other. We are worth the time that we invest in ourselves.

What I have understood is this: the moment you decide to live your life in full accordance with Emotional inclusion whilst allowing your intuition to guide you, it will inevitably take you a step closer to where you need to be. So, if you are sitting back in reservation, hesitation, or fear of opening up about that which you are going through, allow me to gently and ever so kindly snap you out of this frame of mind. Pain is what gives us the opportunity to grow. Pain is universal, but suffering in silence is optional.

Embracing Storytelling

These stories of pain, struggle, survival, recovery, faith, and hope are what tie us together in our joint humanity. The mere fact of incorporating them in the book feels good. We all seem to live in our Emotional silos and forget to remember that we are all cut out of the same cloth. I have said it before, and I will repeat it: it is the school of life for everyone. Failing to admit this in the workplace is denigrating the very humanity of the people we employ. Imagine if all companies were to have a platform where their employees could feel safe to share their stories too. Imagine if all companies were emotionally inclusive enough to be receptive to these stories with zero repercussions. Sharing our stories is a powerful and

Emotional process. It is a part of our inner selves that we reveal, a piece of our vulnerability that we give away. If organizations learn to navigate this with care and respect, it will indisputably encourage a psychologically safe culture, one of belonging, one where employees feel safe in the knowledge that they will not be penalized for expressing their feelings at work. It will indisputably encourage Emotional inclusion. This is powerful.

I hope that this chapter has achieved three things. Firstly, that it has dispelled the myth that the lives of senior leaders are put together and devoid of hardships. We are all walking this earth, living a human experience that spares no one from the hurdles it throws our way. People falsely assume that such leaders have risen to their positions by being profit- and productivity-driven, and that their tenacity to tackle whatever came their way has been spared. Yet the stories of these corporate leaders—including my own—shed light on the humanity that lies within us all, and show how we are all human beings, suffering from the silent stigma against mental health being perpetuated at the workplace, one that calls for men to be stoic and women to avoid being emotional. The truth is that senior leaders, too, struggle. No matter where we sit in the corporate hierarchy, we are all going through the school of life.

Secondly, that it has proven Emotional inclusion is not an airy-fairy concept. But that it is, rather, an increasing area of concern, and direly needed in organizations. In our modern world of work, to be a good leader, and a true leader, one has to be emotionally inclusive. To put people first and to allow ourselves to be vulnerable. As these stories demonstrate, there are leaders out there who want to change the status quo and who are not buying into antiquated organizational thinking about what a leader should behave like. Bold and brave, they are makers of change. And they unveil the powerful change we can create in the world if leaders are on board with Emotional inclusion.

Lastly, I trust that these personal anecdotes illustrate the importance of storytelling, vulnerability, and advocacy for mental health issues amongst leaders. As people who wield substantial influence in organizations, leaders have a voice, a moral obligation, and an ethical duty to speak up. Because unless they boldly and bravely use their voice, and unless they have the courage to call out stigma and confront the issue, the Emotional inclusion revolution for Emotional wellness will not take place at work.

Let us nevertheless be clear that Emotional inclusion is not just for leaders. It also involves us all, whether we are just starting corporate life or are at any other given stage of our workplace journey. The next chapter will further delve into the perspectives of regular workers and how Emotional inclusion can touch us all.

Key Takeaways

- It is only sensible that we view strong, ethical, inclusive leadership as a by-product of Emotional inclusion. If Emotional inclusion is so direly needed in organizations, then in modern times, a good leader must also be one who is emotionally inclusive, who puts people first, and takes the lead in being vulnerable and speaking up about their humanness. Storytelling, vulnerability, and advocacy for mental health or Emotional wellness are key ways leaders can build an emotionally inclusive culture.

- People may falsely assume that senior leaders have risen to high positions by being profit- and productivity-driven, but as humans, they struggle as well. Many of them draw on their own experiences of pain, grief, and loss to inform their ethical leadership ethos.

- There are leaders out there who want change and who already grasp that life involves more than the workplace.

These individuals exercise intellectual humility in their willingness to be less concerned about their priorities in favour of respecting their people's needs, and are able to utilize both their intellect and their emotions to lead well.

- Good leaders have strong moral codes that drive them to create inclusive environments. They focus on communicating and listening and tend to place positive psychology at the heart of their leadership. They are most likely to find Emotional inclusion an important and urgent priority.

- Conversely, weak leaders do not advocate for the mental and Emotional wellness of their people. They do not allocate sufficient budgets for mental or Emotional wellness initiatives and perpetuate vicious systems where staff who speak up about their emotions are penalized or pushed out of their jobs. These leaders will ultimately pay the price in staff turnover.

- In times of upheaval, as people who wield substantial influence in organizations, leaders have the lion's share of responsibility to drive organizational change. They have a voice, a moral obligation, and an ethical duty to call out mental health stigma and confront the issue. Those who do stand out and show the potential change we can create if leaders are on board.

Part V

The Humanization of Work

'The organization of the future would be one where the purpose is front and centre, where the culture is healthy and Emotionally inclusive.'[77]

—DR AMY C EDMONDSON

Thus far, we have covered substantial ground on the topic of Emotional inclusion. Chapters I to III set the stage for what Emotional inclusion is, expounded on the need for a new system around how we handle mental health or Emotional wellness at work, and addressed the stigma around mental health. Chapter IV provided personal insights from industry leaders on the subject of Emotional inclusion and its importance in their lives and organizations.

This chapter, as you will notice, is much longer than the others in the book. The reason being: it goes deep into many,

---

[77] Edmondson, Amy C. (2022, August 19) 'Emotional Inclusion x Amy Edmondson: When Psychological Safety & Emotional Inclusion Come Together', *Emotional Inclusion Podcast*, https://podcasts.apple.com/ph/podcast/ei-x-amy-edmondson-when-psychological-safety-emotional/id1518433002?i=1000576545085.

many personal stories, not just those of business leaders, but of everyday people for whom Emotional inclusion is most likely to be beneficial. I have come to realize just how many still have trouble framing the meaning and the importance of humanizing the workplace. These stories help to illustrate the reality of workplace environments today and highlight just how much we are 'humans at work'.

Humans at Work

Dr George Lawton was right when he said, 'Too many of us who die at forty are not buried until seventy'.[78] Allegorical, no doubt, yet you will have to admit, the way we think and live our lives is completely distorted. We fail to show up fully and authentically. The rigid conformity of our society leaves so many of us running about our to-dos and clocking-in and clocking-out of work to survive. I personally find this robotic culture on steroids nothing short of sad. Depression, stress, and burnout are vastly overlooked, and as we have already covered, absenteeism, turnover, and lack of engagement are direct consequences of that. We have somehow forgotten about the place for 'joie de vivre' in our lives and at work, the very life force of what ignites our humanness.

One of the largest workplace studies in 2022 found that unfair treatment at work was the biggest source of burnout, followed by an unmanageable workload, unclear communication from managers, lack of manager support, and unreasonable time pressure[79]. We still have a very fragmented and splintered work

---

[78] Lawton, George (1947, January 12) 'Sayings of the Week', Page 6, Column 6, *The Observer*.

[79] 'State of the Global Workplace Report', 2022, Gallup, retrieved February 24, 2023, https://www.gallup.com/workplace/349484/state-of-the-global-workplace-2022-report.aspx.

landscape to break through in the aftermath of COVID-19, which utterly floors me. This is no watercooler talk. The workplace of today needs actionable change. It is not enough to be unfailingly kind, compassionate, empathetic, etc. What can we do preventatively, so that it sounds more palatable psychologically? The subject matter is still very unvarnished.

I have heard very few discussions where people admit this. On the contrary, many are diving back into the rat race. I see so many people sweeping the life lessons they have learned or re-learned during the lockdown under the old same dusty carpet of conventional thinking and doing. As companies get back to business as usual and strive for a return of the old order of work, many employees have simply reverted to their old habits of work, without questioning them or taking into account the new lessons learned about the need for human connection and work–life balance brought to light by COVID-19. Instead, they are working longer hours, taking on more projects, and brandishing renewed busyness and overflowing schedules as badges of honour.

Perhaps it is simply that people have no choice in the matter but to get back to work. As the world reopens and businesses shift gears from crisis management back to profit mode, many are striving to make up for losses, and lost time. In turn, staff find themselves back on the hamster wheel, swept along by the momentum to meet key performance indicators. To cope with the heavy load, people are almost mechanically diving back in, working longer and harder. Old habits die hard. We are hardwired to revert to the familiar, even if the familiar is a toxic, result-driven work culture we had been numb to pre-pandemic.

Here, it may be tempting to blame leaders for not being able to strike a balance between mental wellness and getting things done, for adopting a 'go, go, go, go' attitude in response to pressures to get business back up and running. But leaders themselves are not exempt from the negative effects of toxic approaches to work.

I hear so many C-suites telling me that they are exhausted, sending me one-liner emails, not out of rudeness, but out of genuine lack of time. Many leaders, too, have had no opportunity to transition back into work post-pandemic. Instead, they have been thrown back into hyperdrive without any lag time and with an additional layer of stress from trying to seize opportunities for their teams and people as business returns with a vengeance. Many leaders are going through with it without any awareness of the toll it is taking on their lives, psyches, and well-being. Not everyone is complaining, but they are all under more pressure than before.

The truth is that the pandemic has changed us, whether or not we wish to return to our old ways. It has changed our behaviours and the way we work, and allowed us to revaluate our priorities, whether in our families or careers. And in the current 'shadow pandemic', as we navigate our way out of the effects of COVID-19, we need to make our workplace a place of growth?. We are living in a new era, where our duty is to breathe creativity and humanity into work. Old management paradigms brought into the 21st century will simply no longer do; now we need Emotionally inclusive environments, ones where human experiences are co-created to drive balance and results.

There is very evidently a waking-up of consciousness, if I may, within the realm of the workplace. It is, however, very staggered and unintegrated. There is no humanistic roadmap for employers and employees on how to show up in this new landscape's reality we are living in now. How should our workplaces become places of growth? How might Emotional inclusion play out in the workplace of the future? What exactly must we do to be emotionally inclusive?

My answer is that Emotional inclusion is a code of being. And to help more people get on board, we need to spell out the behaviours that have to take place. I break down the elements of Emotional inclusion into the following areas:

- Solidarity
- Prevention
- Kindness
- Flexibility
- Vulnerability
- Empathy
- Compassion
- Listening
- Trust
- Confidentiality
- Purpose

The next sections will delve into each of these areas and explore just how to embody them at work. Some sections will also feature personal anecdotes to further illustrate the reality of the situation—and perhaps inspire others to take up the Emotional inclusion mantle.

Solidarity at Work

The scale of human suffering that the pandemic brought on is unparalleled. Millions are still grieving the loss of their loved ones. We see that people, and especially the Millennials and Gen-z *(the generation of tomorrow),* are revaluating what it means to be happy at work. The world has changed; shall we put this on repeat so that we all hear it, integrate it, and move forward authentically with it? The toll of stress, anxiety, and depression are off the charts.

In light of this, solidarity is one integral component of the humanization of the workplace of the future. Merriam-Webster defines solidarity as 'unity that produces or is based on a community of interests, objectives and standards'[80]. So, you

---

[80] 'Solidarity', Merriam-Webster, retrieved February 24, 2023, https://www.merriam-webster.com/dictionary/solidarity.

might now ask what solidarity looks like in the workplace—which would be a valid question. Where is the 'us' component? What are the concepts, levels, and challenges? Let us break it down.

The 'us' component is essentially the 'bonding element', that which ties the organization's culture together—the recognition of what must be done and educating ourselves on the emerging trends are of essence. One could argue that our understanding of solidarity in the post-pandemic world has changed, and we are now called to frame things differently and reconstruct new forms of solidarity in ways in which we can compare and measure results. We all know the famous adage 'what gets measured, gets done'. Looking at solidarity today in the workplace is an issue of inclusion and exclusion. Wouldn't you agree? We all have unique and individual experiences—expecting each other to think, act, and respond in the same way that we would is flawed and oftentimes drives us to false biases. I would beg to say that new emotionally inclusive solidarities should be at the centrefold of our business agendas if we want our people to feel unified, engaged, and whole at work. There is still so much for us to do.

One thing to note is that solidarity is not the same as unity. In examining the differences between these terms, Charley Richardson, who formerly directed the 'Labor Extension Program' at the University of Massachusetts-Lowell, notes that 'when worker solidarity exists, people are united by much more than connection to leaders or to a program'[81].

Unity, he says, seeks to build connections between workers and the union—in our case, the organization—while solidarity focuses on building connections between co-workers, accepting that not all of them will feel connected to the organization.

---

[81] Richardson, C. (2010) 'Working Alone: Protecting and Building Solidarity in the Workplace of the Future' [Paper 4], *Labor Resource Center Publications*, retrieved February 24, 2023, http://scholarworks.umb.edu/lrc_pubs/4.

'People can unite behind a person or a program', he writes, 'but this does not replace the fundamental solidarity that is a stronger, more visceral reaction growing out of social connection.'

What does this mean? That solidarity is the binding glue amongst individuals in an organization. It goes beyond promoting connections towards the company DNA. The nucleus of solidarity is found through authentic, purposeful, shared action. Solidarity occurs when employees unite around a value that strikes a chord with them—whether that is mental health or Emotional wellness at work, sustainability, organizational values, or more—and find a joint meaning, as a collective, in not just the betterment of their lives but also the betterment of the corporate culture as a ripple effect.

The feeling of belonging to a greater purpose is what makes solidarity a part of Emotional inclusion. Solidarity is taking a collective approach to changing the lives of workers for the better in a sustainable way.

Prevention at Work

Karishma Tulsidas, Content Strategist & Founder, Contente

A single message can change your entire life. It was a Thursday afternoon when a friend-cum-ex-colleague asked me whether I was quitting my job, because she had just been approached by a headhunter for my position—a position that I was still holding and one that I had no intention of leaving. At the risk of sounding clichéd, it was a punch in the gut.

I had been at the company for one year as the head of the editorial department in Singapore. It had been a trying year as I was recovering from severe burnout and overcoming grief from a series of losses in my personal life. I was not okay, mentally and emotionally, and I knew that my performance had been impacted. Still, I was rolling with the punches to perform efficiently, hit targets, and manage the team effectively.

To hear that I was being replaced came as a shock because my company had never conducted a feedback session with me. My knowledge of where I stumbled comes from my own self-awareness, rather than any constructive feedback. A few months prior to this incident, I had reached out to my managing director. This was during one of the COVID lockdown periods, and I told her I was struggling mentally and emotionally for reasons I was not comfortable disclosing. She did not ask, and I did not say.

While she was empathetic, there was no follow-up, neither was there a discussion about how I could be supported. Shortly after, she quit the job, and her role was filled internally. Instead of promoting the long-standing sales director, they made her jump through hoops to prove herself by giving her the title of 'acting managing director'.

That is when things started unravelling. As the new acting managing director, she had a lot to prove. And I became the punching bag. The role was challenging, I will not lie. It was not the first time that I was leading a team, but this team was bigger and cross-functional, and I also had a dotted reporting line to our regional headquarters. I often felt out of my depth, and I remember often shaming and blaming myself and constantly feeling I was not good enough.

But hindsight brings insight. Looking back, I know now that feeling like you are drowning, or that you have zero guidance and support, is not normal. While everyone who climbs the ladder knows that each step upward comes with uncertainties and challenges, feeling out of your depth for such an extended period of time is often the result of an unsupportive, toxic environment. When companies invest in people, they invest in their success and growth. Nobody comes as a pre-packaged superstar. This ascent to success requires training, workshops, a healthy cycle of feedback and critiquing, and the space and compassion to make mistakes. Importantly, throughout the process, you want to be treated like a human being.

The acting managing director started micromanaging me and my team. It was to such an extent that our regional headquarters would contact her instead of me to ask for updates. While I empathize with her insecurity, it does not negate the fact that micromanagers often do more harm than good.

There was one particular incident when headquarters asked her to ask me to send them a list of the individuals we were interviewing for a massive region-wide project. This was on a Wednesday, and I was still awaiting some confirmation. I replied that the list would be sent to them on Friday, or latest on Saturday. On Friday, before I had even had the chance to compile the list, I received an email from headquarters, demanding a response. In the email, I was called unprofessional for not responding to them on Wednesday—my manager had clearly not conveyed my message— and they cast doubt on my professionalism and my credentials. 'If you cannot convince these individuals to be interviewed, then you're lying about the relationships you said you have.'

After a heated back-and-forth, I found myself at the losing end of the argument, mostly because I had had the gall to argue back. Instead of ironing out the situation, the acting managing director called me a few days later and shouted at me for a good ten minutes. Funnily enough, I was able to glean some valid points about how I could have managed the situation better, but the damage had been done. Shouting at a colleague, that too a manager in your team, is not conducive to success; instead, it builds up walls and defence systems, as well as resentment.

Emotional inclusion happens when companies treat their employees with fairness and empathy, and gives them a space where they feel heard, understood, and dignified.

At one point, I was being pressured by the acting managing director to force my team to work overtime and on weekends so the company could save money on freelancers. The team had already been working incredibly hard (and hitting targets), so I pushed back, revealing that I had gone through burnout before and hence did not feel it was ethically right to push my team over their limit. She replied, 'Maybe I am just more resilient than you.' Another incident involved a company-wide email from the local CFO, urging teams to clear their leaves before year-end but pleading with them to continue working because of 'deadlines'.

These seemingly small incidents were telling. There was no allowance for open conversations about mental health or burnouts, and there

> *was no space to not be okay, even during the pandemic. This kind of rhetoric made me feel like I had to suck it up, and my vulnerability could potentially be used as a weapon against me. I felt alone, lost, and started shaming myself. After I left, I realized that it was a form of gaslighting, as I was made to believe that no matter how hard I worked, it would never be enough.*
>
> *I wish that I had been given the space to have an open, honest dialogue. I wish that management saw situations not through the lens of their limited experience, but through a macro perspective that allowed them to give concessions to different personalities and different situations. I wish that there were frameworks in place where feedback was given on a regular basis, rather than a yearly, perfunctory review. I wish that there had been access to programmes, workshops, and training to learn the soft skills that one needs to develop as one climbs the ladder.*
>
> *After I received my friend's message, I quit my job. I closed that chapter of my life with a choice: to believe my company's actions and that I was not good enough or believe in myself and celebrate my achievements rather than failures. The latter was a much harder choice but one that I believe was the better one.*

We have spoken about solidarity, and now I would like to tackle the need for prevention in our efforts to humanize our work landscape. Here, I specifically would like to laser-focus on looking at the concept of 'false assumptions,' for when promoting solidarity, we need to be cautious of them, as they act as barriers that prevent connection between people. And humans, unfortunately, are hardwired to make false assumptions about people or jump to conclusions, as evolutionary psychology shows. In an article for *Harvard Business Review*, Emeritus Professor of Organizational Behaviour at London Business School, Nigel Nicholson writes: 'Although human beings today inhabit a thoroughly modern world of space exploration and virtual realities, they do so with the ingrained mentality of Stone Age hunter-gatherers'[82]. 'Homo sapiens emerged on the Savannah Plain some 200,000 years ago, yet according to evolutionary psychology, people today still seek those traits that made survival possible then: an instinct to fight furiously when threatened, for instance, and a drive to trade information and share secrets', he adds. 'Human beings are, in other words, hardwired. You can take the person out of the Stone Age, evolutionary psychologists contend, but you cannot take the Stone Age out of the person.'

What does this all mean? Understanding psychology, to some measure, is useful for leaders to rethink the humanization of work. While our emotions are primal, we must err on the extreme side of caution in how we interact with each other, as we really do have the moral obligation to practice acute self-awareness in how we choose to navigate our social connections.

There is no question that making false assumptions can be offset through active and unfiltered communication. But let us be clear, this is not enough. Creating a non-judgmental cultural mindset that fosters prevention rests in always keeping an inquisitive mind. When in doubt, always question, versus jumping to a conclusion.

Take Karishma, for example, who was unfairly and 'conveniently' dismissed from her role for having spoken up about her burnout and being mentally and emotionally drained. Not only was there no communication in-and-around the matter, neither was there any proper follow-up as to why she was being replaced. There is no doubt that false, uneducated assumptions were made about her by the organization, and it begs the question: how could this unfortunate event have been prevented?

Stories like Karishma's run rampant in companies today as false assumptions loom large. Take another scenario, one employee

---

[82] Nicholson, N. (1998, July–August) 'How hardwired is human behavior?' *Harvard Business Review*, retrieved February 24, 2023, https://hbr.org/1998/07/how-hardwired-is-human-behavior.

who leaves at 6 p.m. on the dot every day versus one that stays on till much later—the question of which employee is the most dedicated or hardworking begs to be debated. On the one hand, the employee leaving early might have to get home earlier to help his or her children with homework, yet, on the side, they will continue to answer emails or be connected on their phones for work (or not, which is perfectly fine too.) The employee staying in late might be spending more time in the office, but working on personal matters, such as their next vacation. Or take the example of an employee who has been looking unmotivated and lethargic. A response to this would be to think that the said employee is not taking his or her job seriously, when perhaps he or she might be going through some deeper personal issue that they are struggling to cope with. Assumptions are dangerous and counter-productive to an emotionally inclusive culture. Why? Because taking anything as a fact without proof is powerfully dangerous. No one is a mind reader. We need to train ourselves to be very pragmatic in terms of how we choose to think and perhaps always choose to see positive intentions first (at least until proven wrong).

We have all been guilty of making assumptions only to find out later that we were wrong. Prevention is awareness at work. It is both the cure and the answer to moving the needle of mental health at work in the right direction. Stereotyping race, gender, age, sexual orientation, education level, household income or Emotional state cannot be allowed. Unless leaders destigmatize authentic communication, there will be no advancements in the arena of Emotional inclusion. We perpetuate toxic workplaces by forming opinions too quickly and by not addressing clichés that feed the myths. Pervasive clichés, such as people with mental illnesses cannot be well-integrated into the workplace or successful, could not be further from the truth.

Lyn Lee's story in Chapter IV is a perfect example of this. Does living with a mental health condition make you any less well-performing in the workplace? Judging from her corporate success as the Global Head of DEI at Shell, the answer is evident. Drawing mindfulness and creating alertness around these themes call for change through action-driven policies. Preventative awareness leads to sustainable change.

Creating emotionally inclusive organizational pillars is vital to managing the wellbeing of our workforce. Assumption is deadly when it comes to motivation, productivity, and bottom line. Providing an employee assistance programme where free psychological consultations are offered to employees, or training employees to be mental health or Emotional wellness diplomats as first care respondents, or even creating a platform that caters to the global health and safety of employees are ways to prioritize the humanistic business ethos. As discussed in the earlier chapters, unless we put our people first and at the very centrefold of our organizational agendas, we will continue to play silent parts in perpetuating a workplace devoid of humanness.

Kindness at Work

People would never guess in a million years that I am currently going through the heartache of a divorce. It is such an internal tsunami that I am living through, and while I am equipped with the psychological tools to cope, it still does not take away the fact that my emotions dictate how I feel. The random acts of kindness that have come my way, without my disclosing my personal life, have touched me to my core. I cannot stress the value of kindness enough. Defined as the quality of 'being generous, helpful, and caring about other people'[83], kindness is assistance or concern for others, without expecting reward. And, I will add, kindness is the ability to put our humanity at the centre of our social connections.

---

[83] 'Kindness', Cambridge Dictionary, retrieved February 24, 2023, https://dictionary.cambridge.org/dictionary/english/kindness.

Real change starts with conscious and educated leadership, stemming from kindness at its core.

Kindness to me is such a fundamental pillar of what good leadership should embody. It is powerfully transformative. Studies left, right, and centre demonstrate that kindness benefits organizations across a suite of key business metrics, including higher productivity, increased engagement, higher customer satisfaction, and lower turnover[84].

Truth be told, I am not surprised. Kindness catalyses Emotional inclusion and belonging, which are powerful in themselves, yet perhaps what we fail to remember is that the 'returns' always outgrow the act itself. Truth be told, I am always continuously surprised by the active reminders we must set when it comes to this arena; as if kindness were a soft, unimportant skill within the realm of the workplace. The prevailing toxic behaviour of treating each other as robots, devoid of emotions, to 'perform' and get things done has been the status quo. And yet, what we know of each other's lives is so incredibly restrictive that failing to be kind is, to me, simply not an option.

There is a plethora of ways in which we can foster kindness in the workplace. It still frankly completely baffles me that we are still having to spell this out. An honest compliment goes a very long way. But pay attention: the move to online work has removed the chance of 'serendipitous encounters', such as giving a compliment, or saying a 'thank you for great work' as you pass someone in the hallway or share a lift together[85]. This means

---

[84] Sezer, O., Nault, K., & Klein, N. (2021, May 7) 'Don't Underestimate the Power of Kindness at Work', *Harvard Business Review*, retrieved February 24, 2023, https://hbr.org/2021/05/dont-underestimate-the-power-of-kindness-at-work.

[85] Sezer, O., Nault, K., & Klein, N. (2021, May 7) 'Don't Underestimate the Power of Kindness at Work', *Harvard Business Review*, retrieved February 24, 2023, https://hbr.org/2021/05/dont-underestimate-the-power-of-kindness-at-work.

we need to work a little harder to replace the lost 'water-cooler moments' with the help of technology.

How can we do this? Examples include:

- Adding a human touch to online meetings with 'kindness rounds'. At the start of virtual meetings, each attendee shares something caring that someone present around the table or present on the virtual call has done. I often share a personal story with my team before diving into proper business. This switches the focus away from simply our cognitive abilities and analytics and strategizing skills to our softer attributes.

- Using emojis in online chats. Not being afraid to show emotion in business conversations brings our humanity to the fore.

- Reaching out to employees virtually to set a date to catch up on a one-on-one basis offline.

We are social creatures, and we all need to be validated through affirmation and attention. Organizations that know how to foster this, whether online or offline, are shown to arguably be more successful. Why? Well, because an employee who feels recognized and validated will always pay it back. Kindness stretches far beyond compliments to the entire spectrum of showing concern for others, whether by expressing empathy and being a good listener, or simply giving a smile to someone you walk past. You might also consider giving a helping hand to a colleague when you see others are hesitant or unwilling. My personal favourite is carving out time out every week to help a colleague, friend, or stranger who has reached out via LinkedIn, email, or referral. No matter how overloaded my schedule is and no matter how time deprived I am, I make it a priority. What I get out of doing this, humanly speaking, is powerful. I always learn something, create a connection, feel valued—which in turn makes me feel good—and obtain a new perspective. As Winston Churchill said, 'We make a living by what we get. We make a life by what we give'.[86] He could not have been more on point.

When we enable an organizational culture of collaboration and innovation through kindness, we allow a space for our humanity to shine. We effectively change the dry ecosystem of work into one where employees can feel valued and seen. If people truly are at the heart of every business, then fostering kindness brings the 'heart' back into doing business.

The beauty of kindness is that it is contagious too! Researchers from Stanford found that when people see someone else being kind, they are more likely to act kindly towards others themselves[87]. It is also good for your health, mind you. Kindness causes the brain to release oxytocin, a neurotransmitter responsible for feelings of connectedness and trust that facilitate interpersonal bonding. 'It's like a filial response that we have physically. By increasing oxytocin, we can experience a connectedness with kin, essentially', psychiatrist Marcie Hall said in a podcast for American Health Organization University Hospitals[88]. According to Hall, kindness is cardioprotective: it lowers blood pressure, strengthens the immune system, and leads to longer life and higher self-esteem. Caring for our own well-being and caring for the well-being of our co-workers undeniably calls for kindness. This is a key component to being emotionally inclusive, one that I live by as a golden rule.

---

[86] Churchill, Winston, as quoted on the Winston Churchill Trust website, https://www.churchilltrust.com.au/churchill/.

[87] Nook, E.C., Ong, D.C., Morelli, S.A., Mitchell, J.P., & Zaki, J. (2016, August) 'Prosocial Conformity: Prosocial Norms Generalize Across Behavior and Empathy', *Personality and Social Psychology Bulletin*, 42(8), 1045–1062. Sage Journals, retrieved February 24, 2023, https://journals.sagepub.com/doi/10.1177/0146167216649932.

[88] 'The Science Behind Kindness and How It Benefits Your Health', University Hospitals, retrieved February 24, 2023, https://www.uhhospitals.org/blog/articles/2020/10/the-science-behind-kindness/. (2020, October 8).

Flexibility at Work

Anonymous

I was working for this leading luxury group for two decades when a new challenge was offered to me within one of its prestigious brands. I loved that group, I always felt happy working for its high-end brands in a rich environment surrounded by great colleagues—some of them I am still friends with after more than twenty years! So I remember feeling content and confident while accepting this opportunity, while knowing this particular brand's company culture and business requirements were complex and tough. My years of service and experience convinced me that I should be successful by adapting quickly to my new environment and its challenges.

This time, it was different, and I felt from the beginning that there was no human connection or company culture that would reflect the group's 'family-spirit' values. Individual behaviours around values of empathy, humility, and integrity encouraged by the group were totally absent.

It started with little things . . . a tone of voice sometimes bossy, angry, nasty, or abusive, then repetitive calls at night, weekends, during leave. Long hours were a daily routine for all. Everyone in the company got the same treatment—management by fear—given from the boss. And as he was the 'boss', we would have to follow his lead and adapt to his abusive style. We were all suffering in silence.

As a manager myself, I had the duty to protect my team from an over-pressuring boss, but that did not always work as I wanted. With much effort, I tried to explain his behaviour—finding him excuses sometimes—and giving my own guidance and care to the team. However, after a few months of 'bad treatment' and intense Emotional suffering, colleagues would quit. Some were burnt out, and all were tired of being badly treated, despite working round the clock for an organization that was pressuring them to the highest point. Staff turnover was the highest in the group and HR was well aware of the reasons behind it.

When giving HR feedback, or asking for their support, they would reply using the same sentence: 'This is how it works with this brand and this boss, we cannot change the culture, you need to find your own way.'

At first, I was really thinking I could survive this harsh environment, as I would convince myself I was over it and nothing was personal, it was only professional. One night, after a long and stressful day at work, the HR manager burst into tears in my arms because of the accumulated pressure from management, revealing how 'toxic the environment was'. It was a shock to me to hear this from the HR manager herself.

Little by little, I realized the toxic environment was also affecting me, my confidence, my critical thinking, and the quality of my work. As my stress level increased, my sleep was affected, and I became very angry at myself for not being able to take a step back and realize that the one responsible for the way I felt was sitting in the big office.

As I was slowly but surely losing my confidence, it gave him more power over me to insult me, to tell me what I was doing was 'shitty' and deplorable, as I was struggling to reach my objectives.

I kept everything to myself, having shared issues with HR a few times without any change, until one day I felt so bad I had to go to the doctor, who put me on medical leave for two weeks. This was the beginning of the end. Even during my medical leave, they still contacted me on a daily basis with pressure to deliver my work. Coming back to work after the two weeks, despite sharing my issues once again, no support was given to help me get back on my feet and find solutions to change the office dynamics.

So, I went back to my job as per normal, trying to put limits to protect my own mental health, yet still suffering from the abusive management, and trying to think of my next step to get out of this environment.

A few months later, a trigger accelerated the whole process when I learned of the loss of my best friend after a long illness. Right after getting the terrible news, I was having a meeting with the boss and HR on a business topic . . . so I went into the meeting room, and by the look on my face, they knew something was wrong. I burst into tears and told them what had happened. Without any emotion, my boss told me, 'Sorry for you, we still need to go over some figures quickly and after that you can go home.' And as a stupid sheep, I just stayed and conducted the meeting—in tears—without further protesting.

The same HR manager who had burst into tears a few weeks before was seated in that meeting and did not say anything. That was really the trigger that made me realize that what I was enduring at work was totally wrong and unacceptable. Maybe it was also a sign from my friend, telling me life was too short to accept such a bad treatment.

A month after this incident, I was given a letter of dismissal from the company. They had decided I was not up to the challenge since I had shown signs of weaknesses. I was useless.

Today, I am happy I managed to turn the page and embark on happier paths. Thinking back on what happened a few years ago, I think it would have been a very different story if we had had access to a fully-trained and competent HR team which would have been able to understand, mediate, and support staff distress.

The best step that every company should take is to recognize the importance of Emotional inclusion, not only to acknowledge it, but really 'act' on it. Having a trained, unbiased, and objective professional therapist within the organization would be ideal to not only address but solve those issues and avoid further Emotional distress for so many of us.

Flexibility in our thoughts and actions is important. Flexibility, as I see it in the workplace, is the ability to think outside of the box and adapt. We often tend to live our lives with an odd appropriation of 'the truth' (the ego trap), the so-called 'self-righteousness' we all fall into occasionally. No one has the answers to everything, and when it comes to a more humane workplace of the future, we are called to quite literally forgo all the archaic beliefs to make room for sustainable change. I highlight the word 'sustainable' because we can no longer afford to look at change in any other way. One-offs and quick, band-aid solutions are recipes for failure—we all know this by now, right? The world is in crisis, the workplace is in crisis, the state of *our humanness* is in crisis. This is not an airy-fairy matter. The impetus to pull up a big mirror in front of humanity has never been of greater importance. Albert Einstein once supposedly said, 'I did not arrive at my understanding of the fundamentals of laws of the universe through my rational mind'. When connecting to our humanness at work, this is also a reminder to not forget the realm of the heart too. They are interlinked: our heart, body, mind, and soul are the vibrational frequency we all dance to.

Flexibility in our thinking and doing means pushing boundaries, taking a magical eraser out, and wiping away all the dysfunctionalities of the past to rewrite a new script that spells out positive change. With changing circumstances and expectations, employees are now demanding companies to adapt to a new model of work-life balance. Flexible employers, flexible employees, flexible schedules, flexible workstations, all have one thing in common: they offer benefits. And benefits lead to employee satisfaction, greater retention, greater engagement, and increased loyalty. Benefits meet the needs of both the business and its workers to positively impact the organization at stake.

When we think of flexible benefits for our employees, insurance comes to mind once again. Someone who is going through cancer, for example, and who is confronted with their own mortality, will inevitably, at some level or another, experience some degrees of either clinical or sub-clinical depression. Now, the question begs to be asked: why should their mental coverage not be taken as importantly as their physical coverage of chemotherapy? If the baseline reason is *money/profit*, well once again, let us sit back and soak in our degrees of *moral and ethical flexibility*. We live in a rapidly changing world and we are all called to practice flexibility in questioning the status quo, thereby valuing our humility over pride and curiosity over conviction.

Vulnerability at Work

Anonymous, Academic at a University

I have never been an overtly strategic person, and maybe this will be obvious in the story I am about to share. I was taught to work hard and told that bragging is just poor form. Those who have substance do not need to brag, others will notice their work naturally. I joined academia primarily because I thought that academic work is the one where politics should matter the least, and boy was I wrong! The story I am about to share happened twelve years into my career, all of which I have spent at the same institution.

I submitted my file for an evaluation to be promoted to full professor. In terms of requirements, I felt like I had a very good chance of getting promoted. The requirements regarding research publications, as well as teaching, were based on objective criteria and were easy to measure. I exceeded both of those with flying colours.

Then there was the citizenship report, which evaluated your level of service to the institution. Among a million other commitments, I have been managing a specialization for the past nine years, sponsored by a large company, where we were just renegotiating the contract, where the company agreed to give over $1 million for a multi-year contract. Should I also mention that I had just given birth to my third child, and worked throughout my maternity leave to secure the new contract?

A couple of months go by, and the letter arrives. I am shocked to find out that I am not promoted, but what completely floors me is the reason. In the letter, it read that I am not a collegial person, and that I need to work better together with other professors, staff, and colleagues. This is a slap on my face, one that shakes me to the core. Firstly, anyone who knows me for more than five minutes will understand how untrue that statement is. As an ex-athlete, working in teams and being a good team player were embedded deeply in me. Secondly, because the culture of the institution where I am at is exactly that—not collegial and territorial, with people not sharing—how dare they say something to me about collegiality?

I ask for feedback to understand where this information is coming from, only to find out that there is basically only one data point—a woman in my team who I recruited five years earlier to help replace me in managing the programme when I was on my first maternity leave. She has been working part-time for the programme ever since. I have opened many doors for her at my institution and secured her a part-time position in the programme that I was managing.

Just before I went on my third maternity leave, she asked me for a promotion to a position that would technically replace my role, something I was not comfortable with, as her behaviour was often unpredictable and unprofessional. In addition, I liked my role at the time and did not want to give it up. She used the period that I was away to have my baby to create rumours about me and speak to everyone in my institution that she could access, even the client.

Her behaviour was hurtful to be sure. But I think what I could not believe was how my institution and the dean handled this. Why had nobody come to me and asked me for my side of the story? Why was more information not collected? Why did they not decide to speak to more people who worked closely with me? Did twelve years mean nothing?

After being in disbelief for a few days and talking to a few colleagues, I decided to appeal this decision. Some told me that I was crazy to appeal, that they had never overturned a promotion decision. But I had to appeal for myself. I had to fight it. This was not about the promotion but rather about the story that was not true, and an attack on my character.

At this time, a friend shared with me the video of Brené Brown and her TED talk on vulnerability. I think it was and her and Brené's work that helped me fight through this. I felt that I had to step into the arena to defend myself and my character. I had to be brave and fight. In this place where there were no loyalties, where even proper due process did not exist, I did not want to live with an official document with my name on it describing me as a person who was not able to work with others.

So, I launched my own campaign, submitted an appeal, and asked six colleagues to write letters for me giving their take on what it was like to work with me. I shared my story with everyone who listened. I also asked to present my story in front of the appeal committee, which was probably the most humiliating point of all. Six months after receiving my initial evaluation, I received another call from the dean to tell me that I was promoted, that a new edited letter of evaluation was issued, and to say that they were sorry. They also decided to adopt my process, moving forward, by asking three people to write letters for each person applying for a promotion, making it a more balanced process.

I felt incredibly proud that I had fought for myself and won this battle. But did it cost me . . . I felt like I had gone through a real trauma, which took me months to recover from. I feel like it affected my level of trust in the institution and people that I work with. I am still at the same institution and choosing to be anonymous in my story. Now I have a new role, which requires me to manage quite a lot of people. Even if I am learning every day on how to lead, what happened to me makes me much more cautious about how I treat people. Every day, I choose to listen and to ask questions because I know that this paves the way to Emotional inclusion. We all need to be heard and seen at face value for who we are and how much we have to contribute.

Great power resides in leaders acting on their vulnerability to showcase that their infallibility is not a weakness. That weakness does *not* mean fragility. Rather, it is about showing up authentically and daring to normalize the fact that we all are imperfectly human. What this does in turn is spearhead meaningful and authentic connection where employees can feel more fulfilled and safe to speak up, thereby leading to better work quality output. The Cambridge Dictionary defines 'vulnerability' as 'being able to be easily hurt, influenced, or attacked'[89]. This quality is known as courage, and it is also creativity. American author and researcher

---

[89] 'Vulnerability', Cambridge Dictionary, retrieved February 24, 2023, https://dictionary.cambridge.org/dictionary/english/vulnerability.

Brené Brown also defines vulnerability as 'uncertainty, risk, and Emotional exposure'[90]. And it is exactly that.

It is uncomfortable to be open in a corporate landscape where the culture calls us to be friendly whilst keeping a cool professional distance with colleagues. The question I often get asked by companies is: where do you draw the line to vulnerability at work? How much 'vulnerability-showing' becomes counterproductive, i.e., where do you draw the line with the so-called 'too much information'? The honest answer to that—dependent on the culture of your company—is that you will not know unless you try. It is no doubt a risk to expose oneself to what could be gossip, criticism, ostracization, or worse, being fired. Yet the literature offers little doubt on the benefits of bringing our full selves to work.

Organizational psychologist Adam Grant puts it beautifully when he writes 'projecting perfection protects your ego but shuts people out and stunts your growth. Revealing struggles shows humility and humanity, opening the door to new sources of support and strength'.[91] Being able to reveal our breadth of humanness in the face of struggle (may it be the loss of a loved one, an illness, being a single parent, etc.) has been tied to enhanced feelings of self-worth, increased creativity and innovation, and deeper relationships, all of which benefit us both professionally and personally.

Vulnerability is certainly not the mindset of the typical leader. In our sociocultural norms, it just is not. Why? Well, because, as we all know, most leaders get promoted into their roles because they project confidence and self-assuredness and a positive vision.

---

[90] Brown, Brené (2015) *Daring Greatly*, Avery.

[91] Grant, A. (2021, February 25) 'Vulnerability is not the opposite of resilience. Vulnerability builds resilience', LinkedIn, retrieved February 24, 2023, https://www.linkedin.com/posts/adammgrant_vulnerability-is-not-the-opposite-of-resilience-activity-6771888478247555074-5q-9/.

Whilst these are not bad things in of themselves, we must remind ourselves that the world has changed and rethinking our mental fossils, that is, our outdated preconceptions of what being a leader is all about, is now a necessity.

Perhaps nowhere is the modern executive's leadership conditioning summed up more plainly than in the premise of a paper on vulnerability written by Sandra Corlett, a senior lecturer in Leader Development and Organization Futures at Newcastle University Business School, and Sharon Mavin, a professor, executive coach, and co-founder of hospitality network All Women Welcome. It opens with how the paper 'explores how senior executives learn (not) to be different . . . as part of a business school executive education programme'[92]. In the study, Corlett and Mavin write that executives regulate their emotions to meet others' expectations of a strong leader, yet this 'mask of invulnerability' is 'psychologically and emotionally intense and depleting' to maintain. Vulnerability and self-expression, they write, is disorienting but liberating.

I repeat, 'maintaining the mask of invulnerability to protect themselves is psychologically and emotionally intense and depleting'. For the Emotional needs of employees, encouraging vulnerability in the workplace is unavoidable. It is, thus, no small assumption to make in saying that yes, vulnerability is a by-product of Emotional inclusion. Because they are so afraid of being judged and rejected due to stigma, people spend most of their lives playing roles to showcase that they have it all together. But, as the researchers have found, that is draining. That is adding

---

[92] Corlett, S., Ruane, M., & Mavin, S. (2021, September) 'Learning (not) to be different: The value of vulnerability in trusted and safe identity work spaces', *Management Learning*, 52(4), 424–44, Sage Journals, retrieved February 24, 2023, https://journals.sagepub.com/doi/10.1177/1350507621995816#bibr36-1350507621995816.

much more work for us than being authentic and showing up with all our emotions would entail.

In the story shared by the academic above, being willing to be vulnerable, being willing to speak up about the experience to others, and to highlight the potentially embarrassing fact about being declined a promotion was key to self-advocacy and the eventual righting of the record. Amid the Emotional turbulence of dealing with a negative event, being vulnerable is particularly challenging. But ultimately, I believe that it is during these times that we realize the value of human connection. Life is beautiful, and it is challenging. From personal experience, the moment you talk about life in a vulnerable and sensitive way, people respond. We should be brave. In revealing to others that we do not have our lives together, that we do not have the capability and rigour to deal with our problems, that we cannot fragment our personal from our professional lives, that we are, simply put, *human*, we are doing ourselves and others a moral and ethical favour. Vulnerability encapsulates all aspects of our lives, and learning to be vulnerable in a work context is as important and inseparable as learning to be vulnerable in a social context.

Empathy at Work

Yasmine Khater, CEO & Lead Researcher, Sales Story Method

It was my first day at work. I was so excited. With new clothes and nerves, I felt like it was the first day at a new school. I could not wait to see what this new chapter—the professional one—had in store for me.

The HR manager welcomed me. After my orientation and onboarding, I was introduced to all the different directors. They all got out of their seats and their glass cabins to greet me. I felt valuable and important. From the windows across the office, I admired the incredible Singapore skyline and thought, 'Wow, this must be adulting.'

The HR Manager and I went about doing rounds in the office, where I was welcomed and greeted by everyone. Until we came across my direct manager . . . my boss. Instead of welcoming me (or even saying hi) on my first day of work, she waved her hand dismissively, indicating that she was busy and unavailable. She was the only one who did not say hi.

I did not think much of it at the time. I assumed that she must have been busy. When I eventually reached my desk, I assumed that she would reach out to me if she needed me. I did not want to get in the way of her work. A few minutes later, I received my first email. As I expected, my boss had reached out to me through an email, containing all the tasks that she wanted me to do.

I did not understand most of it. I was unfamiliar with the processes, learning how everything and everyone operated. So, I went over to her cabin and knocked on her glass door, hoping she would clarify the task list.

Without even sparing me a look, she simply said, 'You should already know.'

I felt dumb for asking. Maybe I should have already known.

This was just the start of months of both verbal and psychological abuse. I'd repeatedly hear the phrases 'You're so stupid' and 'This is very poor work, why did you submit it to me?' The lack of empathy and compassion, coupled with the overwhelming gaslighting and bullying, pushed me into a spiral of self-doubt. Nobody else was treated that way. There must be something wrong with me.

Was it because I was raised in a different country? No, surely it could not be that. Was it because I did not look like most people in the office? No, surely it could not be that. Was it because I was brown? No, surely it could not be that.

Eventually, I discovered that she simply did not want me to be there. When I asked why, the HR manager said, 'Because you are Arab.' She went on to share, 'She thinks you were hired because you and one of the Middle Eastern ambassadors share the last name.'

Huh. Not what I expected. That is like thinking all the Smiths and Lims of the world are related.

I soldiered on, hoping that if I stuck around and worked hard, I'd 'earn my keep'. But the bullying got worse. There were several moments when I would find myself in the toilet cubicle, bawling my eyes out.

I told my aunt I wanted to quit, to which she said, 'You're not going to quit because of a bully.' She continued, 'Maybe that's why you were put through five rounds of interviews, instead of the usual two.' I felt even more helpless.

I started to think that maybe, my boss was onto something after all, maybe I was shit, maybe I was not capable, maybe I was not worth it.

She expected me to know everything… to figure out everything on my own. She would never explain anything. I still remember this one time when it got really bad. We were hosting the chairman of the board, and I had to send out an email to the staff regarding the itinerary and what was expected of everyone.

It was 1 a.m., and the chairman would arrive at 8 a.m. Everyone had their hands full, so I made the call and sent out the email. As someone who is dyslexic, I went over the email a dozen times to make sure nothing had slipped through the cracks. But I still made a mistake—a spelling mistake. I did not see it.

The next thing I knew, I woke up to an email from her at 6 a.m. in the morning. She had hit 'reply all' to over 300 employees and highlighted my one spelling mistake, along with the words, 'You are so incompetent.'

I sat up in my bed, crying. Clearly something was wrong with me. I wanted to hide. Maybe if I did not go to work, it would all go away. But the chairman was coming. So, I did not have the luxury of running away. I swallowed my pride and went to work that day. Many of the directors that I had met on my first day came over to see me. They all had seen the email, and wondered if I was okay.

I was not.

Each of them walked over to me, patted me on the back and said they were there for me. Some even offered to mentor me. It was my first experience with empathy at work. That experience taught me that for every toxic leader in an organization, there are always some compassionate ones too. These people may not always know what is going on, but when they do, they can create a ripple effect of Emotional inclusion.

What is incredible is that because of the gesture of those directors that eventful day, I stayed in that company. I decided to ask for help and took up mentorship with several of the leaders. I remained kind to my boss, despite how she treated me. And eventually, her words did not affect me the same way. Her toxic leadership eventually led her to being demoted. And when someone twelve years her junior became her boss, she threw a tantrum and quit.

So, what changed after the day of the chairman's visit, you ask? I had been transformed. I found respite in the empathy they had offered me. I felt valued and important again. I felt safe and seen. I wanted to keep working.

Clearly, I am not alone in feeling this way. According to Businessvolver, 87 per cent of CEOs agree their company's financial performance is tied to empathy[93].

That day was a pivotal moment in my life. It took me on a journey that led me to where I am now. It led me to teach persuasive storytelling without making people feel the way my ex-boss made me feel—vulnerable and insignificant. I know that we always perform better when we feel safe and seen.

This experience is not unique. It is an example that shows the vital need for Emotional Inclusion in the workplace so that everyone can thrive, and we do not lose top talents in the workforce.

---

[93] 'State of Workplace Empathy', 2018, Businessolver.com, retrieved February 24, 2023, https://info.businessolver.com/hubfs/empathy-2018/businessolver-empathy-executive-summary.pdf.

While empathy is a buzzword that we have heard much of and speak a lot about at work, we fail to give it a real platform and to sharpen our understanding of what it looks like when exercised in the workplace. Let us dissect the reason why. The University of California, Berkeley's Greater Good Science Center, which studies the psychology, sociology, and neuroscience of well-being, says researchers of emotion typically use the term 'empathy' to describe an ability to sense other people's emotions, coupled with the ability to imagine what someone else might be thinking or feeling.[94] So, having empathy allows us *to connect* with an employee or colleague in a way that permits us to go beyond the superficial corridor chitchat, or dry, one-on-one, conversational meeting. Empathy could almost also be referred to as our intuitive emotionally inclusive radar in understanding other people's experiences, especially if we have never lived through them ourselves.

Contemporary researchers have suggested that there are two specific types of empathy. The first is *'affective empathy'*, and it refers to the sensations and feelings we get in response to others' emotions. This can include reflecting what that person is feeling, as if you were a mirror of the other person. For example, feeling stressed when you notice another's anxiety or fear. How many of you can relate to feeling uncomfortable, for example, when you are talking to someone who is nervous in your presence? Or feeling tense for that colleague of yours who you know is terrified of public speaking and is nearing that microphone to do a team presentation? I think being aware that this is called 'affective empathy', thus labelling it, allows us to look at ways to tackle it better through defined strategies to put everyone at ease. Take the first scenario I mentioned. Why not use humour to relax the

---

[94] 'What Is Empathy', *Greater Good Magazine*, retrieved February 25, 2023, https://greatergood.berkeley.edu/topic/empathy/definition.

person stressed in your presence as well as relax yourself from the unaccountability of it at the same token? In scenario two, why not take the initiative of clapping for your colleague getting up to do her presentation to let her know that the team is rooting for her?

The second type of empathy researchers have investigated is called *'cognitive empathy'*, sometimes called *'perspective taking'*, which calls on our ability to identify and understand other people's emotions. We can both feel and understand the pain of someone going through loss, sickness, heartbreak, etc., if we have gone through it ourselves. This is powerful in navigating our relationships at work, even if the big fat stigma still looms behind showcasing how we feel in the first place. We have learned to manage our workdays somewhat (if not, very) robotically, biting our tongues rather than expressing ourselves wholly on an Emotional scale. This drives inauthenticity, not just in our relationships in the workplace, but also in the purpose our organizations give out to the world. Companies are made of people, and if our people cannot be emotionally inclusive, what does this say about the company that employs them?

Compassion at Work

Having empathy does not necessarily mean we will want to help someone in need, but it is arguably the first step toward compassionate action. Why the wording 'compassionate action'? Well, as we have defined, empathy is what allows us to take the perspective of and feel the emotions of another person. Compassion, on the other hand, involves the desire to help. It is a strong feeling of sympathy and sadness for the suffering or bad luck of others, and a wish to help them[95].

---

[95] 'Compassion', Cambridge Dictionary, retrieved February 25, 2023, https://dictionary.cambridge.org/dictionary/english/compassion.

Surely, we can all recount a time when we experienced compassion. I certainly do. I notably remember this specific day when one of my employees asked to speak to me in my office. I could tell by the dark circles around her eyes, her ashy complexion, the lack of her usual vibrant smile, and her rounded shoulders that something was very off. I quietly ushered her in and closed the door. She avoided eye contact and scratched her throat as she sat down. She was feeling anxious, sad, and lost—it was palpable. I have been there too and know the feeling. I warmly smiled at her, took her hand, and gently told her that I was there for whatever it was that she was readying herself to tell me.

She grabbed a Kleenex, straightened herself up in her chair, looked at me, and shared that her husband had gambled away all of their money and that they were indebted up to their eyeballs and facing bankruptcy. She began crying and told me that there was more. She was asking for a divorce and had moved back with her mother, with her daughter. I helped her look at her options, accompanied her at the lawyer's several times, and made sure that she stayed emotionally well to keep powering at her job with us.

I am not saying this to reflect how good of a boss I was but rather to remind us all about the power that lies behind empathy. I might not have experienced my partner gambling all our money away, but I certainly know what divorce feels like and I certainly navigated pain in a way where I could see myself in her. It is no small assumption to say that we have all, at one point or another, been in a dark place and where speaking our truth felt both terrifying and liberating all at once. This employee today is happily remarried, and all the debts incurred during her previous marriage have almost been paid back. She is now one of the most engaged and emotionally connected employees to the company, and one of its most passionate advocates, because she was listened to compassionately, helped, and heard in a sensitive and confidential manner.

Compassion brings back to businesses the fact that businesses are all about people. If companies fail to be compassionate, if they fail to inspire an emotionally inclusive culture, employees will be quick to discern that their employer does not have their back. Consider, for example, an acquaintance of mine who opened up to her boss about a sensitive matter and at the end of the conversation was reminded instead of her outstanding tasks and deadlines. Instead of displays of non-compassion that reroute the conversation to work performance or organizational demands, leaders should hold space for employees to speak up when they are struggling, for example, dealing with abortion, or the death of a loved one, and listening to them with compassion and sensitivity about their deep pain. Whichever employee we serve with compassion will surely pay it back a hundredfold.

When we are confronted with another's suffering and feel called to relieve that suffering, magic happens. Make no mistake, this is not 'airy-fairy' magic. As we've discussed, empathy—and by extension, compassion—catalyses the secretion of oxytocin in our bodies, thereby lowering blood pressure, boosting immunity, and increasing calmness. And would not you argue that we need a lot more of this at work? In fact, exercising compassion stimulates the same areas in the brain associated with our drive for core needs such as food, water, and sex, writes mental health advocate Jill Stark for Stanford University[96]. She adds, 'A growing body of research shows that compassion could be the key to improved health, happiness and longevity'.

Is not it crazy that this is not coming to light more? That workplaces are not addressing this? Our companies are made of

---

[96] Stark, J. (2015, April 12) 'Changing the world and ourselves through compassion', Wu Tsai Neurosciences Institute Stanford University, retrieved February 24, 2023, https://neuroscience.stanford.edu/news/changing-world-and-ourselves-through-compassion.

people, so why are we trying to squeeze the very essence out of our employees—that which would have made them more productive? If people are unwell, stressed, or depressed, they will simply be less productive. This is science-backed, data-driven research, and at Emotional inclusion® in the Workplace, I always advocate and promote these findings to drive discussion and change.

Some may not see the link between compassion and bottom-line benefits, but for me the link is clear. The need to focus on and promote compassion is a reminder that our corporate landscape and workplaces are still not progressive, are still stuck in the industrial-era focus on productivity. But emotion and inclusion drive productivity. The action of putting our emotions first as human beings is what drives productivity. And Emotional inclusion is the very action of bringing in pillars of humanity and life into company culture, one that must be based on compassion for others.

Listening at Work

Anonymous
I grew up in the world of investment banking, and twenty years ago empathy was a foreign word. I remember being a pregnant investment banker and a new mother, and not letting up because I felt I had to be the same or better than I had ever been at work. I remember not having other women in my team, and the loneliness of feeling guilty about leaving my baby while the men were oblivious to the struggles of juggling. I remember taking my baby on a business trip in the middle of my maternity leave because there was an urgent deal related issue. I remember saying, 'I am committed to what I do, but my commitment to my child comes first' and getting back blank looks. I remember working during the night (sleep-averse babies will do that to you) and getting through the days somehow, without a single person asking how I was coping with the change in my life. It just was not how things were done. Those 'two children under two' years were hard and an Emotional

rollecoaster, yet no one would ever think to bring it up, and among my male colleagues, there was not even a hint of being able to relate. I remember how one of the more senior female managers, who I held in high esteem, famously stayed on a business call while in labour, and was touted as a superwoman. That was the benchmark. Being tough and delivering (no pun intended), regardless of the situation, was an expectation many of us had to live up to.

The workplace was not somewhere you brought your life to. 'Exposing' your weaknesses—which we now celebrate as 'being vulnerable'—even to other women, was a huge risk. Those were tough times and if I had had an empathetic working environment, I would have weathered them better. There were about four years in my life which were a bit of a blur because days and nights merged into one and I was in high 'doing mode'. I pushed myself to keep up the pace and never let my feelings show. In all fairness, I did not question it then. Discussing emotions was perceived as a negative thing, especially as a woman professional. There was a misnomer that being a financial professional translated to being impersonal, impervious, and indestructible.

I remember the relief I felt when I changed industries, and when I was able to slowly but surely be more authentic and 'whole' in all my interactions. I remember making that transition to being a senior manager and vowing to create a different atmosphere for my team, to be there for them, put myself in their shoes, and leave the door open for all manner of conversations, planned or spontaneous alike. I remember when I realized that despite my best intentions, I was conditioned to respond to high-pressure situations in a certain way, and needed a 'note to self' to step back and put on my empathetic hat.

Happily, things have changed so much since. The journey of a working mother is no less challenging now, but there are so many more seasoned female professionals in finance than there were two decades ago, and there is a lot more empathy in the workforce for what they go through.

Being empathetic is not at odds with productivity or professionalism, it is about humanizing the working environment and permitting us all to be more open to the issues that everyone faces in life. An empathetic response generates reassurance, demonstrates support for what one is experiencing, and is more likely to create trust and transparency in a team. Today I have the privilege of working in an environment where we feel totally empowered to share how we feel and bring all of ourselves to work.

The challenge we face now is quite the opposite. The post-COVID world has spawned a generation of highly sensitized workforce, who expect their managers to be part-time therapists. Empathy alone will not cut it. We need to be active listeners, identify what we can help with and what might merit professional help, adapt our team dynamics to accommodate how introverts may prefer to communicate and demonstrate their own leadership style, create an environment where no one is mocked for sharing their emotions, and where an open expression of concerns is encouraged to stay grounded in each of our realities. We have heightened mental health issues, like anxiety and depression, which are yet to be normalized, and which are so much harder to uncover or accurately diagnose than physical illnesses that manifest more palpably.

Resilience is a good objective, but the path to resilience often involves confronting, embracing, and making peace with the issue itself. That journey needs our world to be a more empathetic place at large.

I was lucky to have a supportive environment at home and a wonderful group of friends who remain my 'rock' to this day, but not everyone has as many alternatives and the workplace is where many people spend most of their time.

The role of the workplace—and it is no longer strictly an 'office'— needs to evolve into a space that enables every individual to play to their strengths and qualities, accept their unique needs, and help them be the best they can.

Emotional inclusion calls for organizations to be more attuned to the rapidly evolving societal changes, the pressures of life, in a more competitive and crowded planet, and the impact it has on young professionals. Organizations need to think beyond the mere physicality of the 'future of work' to provide their teams with a culture that fosters openness, a safe place to be vulnerable, embolden authenticity, and celebrate differences, in order to have the diversity needed for true innovation and to influence how our society evolves.

Listening is an art that can avoid a plethora of miscommunications, misunderstandings, heartache, frustrations, and trauma. Whilst we would all agree that empathy and compassion are key ingredients to mastering this skill, the organizations that *practice* genuine listening, are still too few. Assumptions are made, oftentimes, false ones, and the cycle of damage perpetuates.

Yes, listening is an art that still so few in the workplace know how to perform. Being human at work does not translate to impressing upon others how well we speak, but rather how well we listen. The Greek philosopher Epictetus, born some 2000 years ago, once said, 'We have two ears and one mouth so that we can listen twice as much as we speak'. Truth be told, we have somehow inversed the two, as if our ability to be fully present for what others have to say has been hijacked by our self-imbued distractions.

We all know the saying 'we all want to love and be loved'. Well, the same would apply to 'we all want to listen and be listened to'. Call it a matter-of-fact statement or not, I still deem it fair to assert. The art of juggling the two is one that is learned. Taking the time out to really 'listen' to a colleague or employee at work *(without interrupting and giving your two cents about what they are saying)* can be tremendously powerful, not just in deepening your relationship with the said person, but also in allowing the person who is 'unloading' the opportunity to freely express themselves. Giving our undivided attention whilst deferring judgement is something we all need more practice doing, would not you say so?

Trust at Work

Binu Balan, Founder & Director, B. Connected Pte Ltd

They say trust is the glue that holds our connections with others together. And to me, the gift of connection is cherished like no other. I recently switched careers to become an entrepreneur, after over twenty years of moving up the ranks in fashion and lifestyle retail, the only industry I have ever worked in and known.

And why did I stay in one industry that long? Because of the people. The people who walked through the doors of our stores each day, the people who worked behind the scenes in store windows, shop floors, stock rooms, warehouses, and in the back offices. These humans created a new world every single day for me, and as I progressed into new roles, and moved to countries with bigger responsibilities, it never occurred to me to switch to or be part of another industry. This was my world, and one that I gave first priority to for a good part of those twenty years.

Work brought me from the Middle East to Singapore in 2009. The bustling shopping malls, the streets milling with people—both residents and tourists—and the opportunity to be outdoors were all very refreshing and new to me in many ways. The noticeable difference here was, however, in the work environment and overall work culture. It was interesting and markedly different from the Middle East, where the workforce—and a large part of the management—were all expats; the unity in that diversity was very visible there.

Over the next ten years I had the privilege of growing with some fine organizations led by dynamic and inspirational leaders. I also had the opportunity to unfortunately experience what leadership should not look like. There was the Irish-origin Singaporean boss from my first workplace who remembered to remind me that Singapore is an enforced democracy and hence freedom of thought and speech will not openly be a part of their organizational culture.

Then there was the female manager whose welcome message on day one at work was: do not sabotage me. I was hired by her manager and so the tension was palpable. This was her everyday attitude and leadership style with everyone in the team. The team was used to her shouting at them and being regularly mocked by her. She was unanimously disliked by the entire team, but she brought in the numbers and, so, kept the job.

To me, these were leadership examples of another dimension. The very visible lack of an inclusive culture within these organizations was shocking. I was not used to this flagrant display of power and there were not many I could talk to about it at the time. I was the foreigner, the outlier. I should leave if I do not like the status quo!

Perhaps the biggest disillusionment in my entire career was my time at this famous global sports brand. I was headhunted to join their senior leadership team in the region. Being a big fan of the brand, I was quite thrilled at the opportunity and looked forward to experiencing a world-class work culture, with inclusion and belonging at its core.

But within the office environment, it was once again a sad repetition of the same old story: people of the same race grouping together, conversations mid-meeting slipping into Chinese or Malay. The office clique was in full display, every time. Newcomers and foreigners were often left out during group lunch outings, unless they were one of the bosses. Your true self was not accepted, and you were not allowed to be authentic. Judgements and micro-aggressions were normalized. Most importantly, it did not look like anyone noticed or recognized the distinct and evident lack of an inclusive culture in that company. Moving on from that environment was the best thing that happened to me.

Workplace exclusion has repeatedly appeared in different forms in the course of my career. Many of my fellow foreign colleagues were subjected to it but were not bold enough to speak up about it, and eventually left. I felt angry and disappointed at the inaction from top management, but it also made me even more determined to let my work do the talking first. I was vocal, I asked questions, and I spoke more than the others. And I was sufficiently unpopular because of it. But I was not here for a popularity contest. I had decided when I moved from

> *familiar terrains to the life of an expat that I would rather be right than be popular.*
>
> *I know very well that just because I have been able to overcome this does not mean everyone will. Office ostracism is real; it omits a fundamental social need for belonging. Being on the receiving end of ostracism is painful and demotivating.*
>
> *Allowing one to feel safe and secure in their office relationships underpins trust as the essential component of Emotional inclusion at work. Creating a positive work culture and fostering productive relationships between employees of all levels in an organization, is at the heart of true Emotional inclusion in the workplace.*
>
> *The solution to exclusion has always been, and always will be, inclusion. An emotionally inclusive work culture led by servant leadership—putting the needs of others first and helping people develop and perform as highly as possible—and fostering of psychological safety will be the best workplace legacy we can leave behind for our future generations.*

I was suggesting parking our judgement earlier when it came to skilfully listening, and this is a point I would like to circle back to with you. If we want our people to speak to us within our organizations, we need to make room for trust. Trust breeds workplace engagement, upscaled morale, and a sense of belonging. A global survey of thousands of workers and business leaders around trust levels between employees and management[97] found that one in four workers have left a company because they did not feel trusted. About six in ten employees say a lack of trust affects their career choices, while over half say a lack of trust impacts their mental health or Emotional wellness. Poor trust, the

---

[97] 'Trust in the Modern Workplace: Why is trust still hard to find at work?' The Workforce Institute at UKG, retrieved February 24, 2023, https://workforceinstitute.org/wp-content/uploads/2020/12/Trust-in-the-Modern-Workplace-Final.pdf.

report adds, hurts companies in multiple ways. One, talent pools are smaller, with one in five employees actively refraining from referring friends, family members, or former colleagues to open roles in a firm they do not trust. Two, employees who do not feel trusted are less productive: two-thirds say that the perception of low trust hurts their daily efforts at work.

These statistics powerfully shed light on the fact that *trust should be a given, not earned.* Humanizing our workplace also means putting our employee interests ahead of company profits. Why? Simply because employee wellness is what drives organizational success. We are not reinventing the wheel here, yet the point is that we are still having to debate the issue today.

Binu's story very much reflects the challenges that exist in creating a workplace of trust. Being an expatriate, the social exclusion she endured and the suspicion with which she was regarded by her managers show just how the lack of a trusting environment harms employee morale.

Even as the pandemic spurred firms to work on another kind of trust—trusting staff to perform well despite working remotely—this catalyst for the re-evaluation of the employer–employee relationship has charted little overall progress on the matter. Rachel Botsman, a lecturer on trust in the modern world, touches on the evolution of trust. She explains that 'in any situation, there is a trust giver and a trust receiver, and it's the trust giver that decides whether to give you their trust. Companies may want to control the trust dynamic, but the trust givers—their employees—are the ones with the power. Healthy work environments are predicated on this new, more equitable, power dynamic'.[98] As we have just unpacked, understanding our employees and their needs is crucial to breeding trust and, thus,

---

[98] 'Rethinking trust at work with Rachel Botsman', Podcast on Culture Amp, https://www.cultureamp.com/podcast/trust-in-the-workplace.

overall profitability. So, the question lingers, how to pragmatically nurture trust at work?

Confidentiality at Work

Emotional inclusion is, as we have already mentioned, acting upon integrating our emotions within the workplace in such a way that employees can be fully heard, seen, and cared for. Taking intentional action in understanding the expectations of our employees is a starting block to building trust. Whilst anonymous surveys might be the obvious place to start, employees still tend to question how anonymous they are—even when reading the fine print of the terms and conditions.

Getting meaningful and trusted feedback starts with defining the rules of confidentiality. This is another key missing pillar when it comes to nurturing emotionally inclusive and human-driven company cultures. *Our employees are the barometer of our companies.* How emotionally well they are benchmarks company performance. I have been repeating this for years now and I must confess to feeling like a broken record at this stage. The fundamental underlying problem is that there is such a profound distrust in our organizations today. The 'human' component in our 'human resources' platforms, for example, has been murky at best, mainly leaning in favour of the employer than the employee, when their true role is to be transparent and fair mediators between employees and their organizations.

We need to be clear that HR departments exist to serve the best interests of the organization that hires them. Irrespective of how we look at it, this is a crucial fact to remember when considering the issue of confidentiality. As we have already covered, any organization is only as capable as its employees and so the *duty of care* is paramount. Very often, HR departments will not be able to directly solve issues themselves. Rather, they will be able to give *open advice*, whether it be medical, professional, or emotional.

I see three red flags in this.

1. 'Open advice' right there spells out the limits of the HR vis-a-vis wellbeing confidentiality to help solve issues that employees come to them with.
2. Medical or Emotional advice within our organizations should be handled with extreme care, professionalism, and background-certified training. Unless our HR representatives are equipped with a relevant medical degree, which in most cases they are clearly not, let us be open to understanding that these individuals are simply not equipped to handle an employee who might be clinically or sub-clinically depressed, for example.
3. Unless we strategize confidentiality measures that employees will feel comfortable with—in other words, that they trust—no transformative, emotionally inclusive culture will come about.

If you ask me, a conventional HR department, or 'happiness officers' for that matter, is not the gatekeeper of our employees' Emotional wellness confidentiality. Conventionally speaking, HR departments are tasked to support the development and implementation of initiatives and systems, provide counselling on policies and procedure, be actively involved in recruitment by preparing job descriptions, post ads and manage the hiring process, create and implement effective onboarding plans, develop training and development programs, assist in performance management processes, support the management regarding disciplinary issues, maintain employee records according to policy and legal requirements, review employment and working conditions to ensure legal compliance, etc. But in very few organizations do mental health or Emotional wellness figure in the list through a medical-driven lens.

According to a recently published *Harvard Business Review* article, up to 80 per cent of people will experience a diagnosable mental health condition over the course of their lifetime, whether they know it or not. But almost 60 per cent of employees have never spoken to anyone at work about their mental health[99]. Understanding why that is does not need one to be a neurosurgeon.

We are back to the Emotional wellness stigma issue, yes. It is at the genesis of it all and acts as a wall for employees who wish to talk openly about their treatments and conditions. There are several reasons an employee might not wish to disclose a mental health condition, including:

- Fear of losing their job or missing out on a promotion.
- Worry over co-workers and their managers judging them.
- Risks of being misunderstood.
- Not wanting to be seen as being given special treatment.
- Witnessing harassment or mistreatment of others who have talked about mental health.
- Lack of trust in their organization to help.
- Difficult relationship with their immediate boss.
- Concerns about being shamed.
- Lack of courage or willingness to speak up.

Lack of Emotional inclusion leads to profound distrust. When fear of speaking up is tied to the mishandling of one's humanity, how could it not? Getting through a workday when you are feeling unwell is hard enough. And if you are coping with something you are afraid to share due to confidentiality purposes and an absence of internal medical infrastructure, powering

---

[99] Greenwood, K. (2021, July 30) 'How to Talk About Your Mental Health with Your Employer', *Harvard Business Review*, retrieved February 25, 2023, https://hbr.org/2021/07/how-to-talk-about-your-mental-health-with-your-employer.

through your day makes it that much harder, if not quasi-impossible. Confidential support and treatment for mental health, such as free or subsidized clinical screenings for depression from a qualified mental health professional, therapy or counselling sessions, and health insurance with no or low out-of-pocket costs for depression medications should be provided to all employees as part of their overall health benefits package. Diversity, Equity, and Inclusion departments would also gain in advocating Emotional inclusion through sharing 'self-identification' stories. It must start from the top, and leaders must take the lead in sharing their own personal journeys of hardship in order to infuse an acceptance of our humanity at work.

The famous quote 'it's okay to not be okay' is not one we hear many CEOs and managing directors openly and authentically voicing out. It might sound good to say it, but how many walk their talk? Within the business world, it is high time that we start prioritizing self-worth over net worth. To do this, we need to look at what our beliefs are in the realm of what successful workplaces look like in order to know what to change. You cannot properly clean your house if the target points of dirt and grime are not identified. It is the same thing here.

We are currently going through a big transition in the workplace, and the pandemic has greatly aided in this need for revaluation, re-invention, and ditching of old, archaic ways. What we can do as a collective of leaders in this realm is powerful. I know that I am not the only one wanting to create a world where it is safe for us to bring our full selves to work. This is partly why I launched the Emotional inclusion podcast, where I host global leaders who are advocates for mental health or Emotional wellness and Emotional inclusion in the workplace. My guests share their own personal challenges and openly disclose the loopholes of our current outdated system. Transparent communication is the birthplace of destigmatization. And we need a lot more of it as mental health is set out to be the biggest challenge of the century, with depression said to become the leading cause of disability and premature death. The Emotional inclusion podcast is here to shatter the status quo and lead the way to a wholesome new mindset in the workforce. The conversations I have are deeply humbling and purposeful to say the very least.

Purpose at Work

Nurturing a deep sense of purpose where personal values and organizational goals align is a by-product of Emotional inclusion. It takes being responsive to the Emotional aspirations of our employees to tap into our understanding of their purpose. McKinsey recently published an article titled 'Help your employees find purpose—or watch them leave'[100]—I cannot help but chuckle at the refreshingly honest and punchy title—in which it outlines how employees expect their jobs to bring purpose to their lives. Employers who fail to meet this need should be prepared to lose talent to other companies that will. The Great Resignation and the Silent Resignation were—and to some degrees still are—perfect reminders of this. What comes out loud and clear is that when employees feel that their purpose is aligned with the organization's purpose, benefits such as stronger employee engagement, heightened loyalty, and a greater willingness to recommend the company to others take centre stage.

McKinsey's research found that 70 per cent of employees said that their sense of purpose is defined by their work. It also found that employees are five times more likely to be excited to work at a company that spends time reflecting on the impact it

---

[100] Dhingra, N., Samo, A., Schaninger, B., & Schrimper, M. (2021, April 5) 'Help your employees find purpose—or watch them leave', McKinsey, retrieved February 25, 2023, https://www.mckinsey.com/capabilities/people-and-organizational-performance/our-insights/help-your-employees-find-purpose-or-watch-them-leave.

makes in the world. This serves as a strong reminder to us that company leaders play a fundamental role in helping employees find their purpose and live it. But here is the catch: how much time do companies vest in authentically engaging with their employees to understand what would make their jobs more meaningful? This is an obvious rhetorical question to which we already know the answer. Spending time with our teams to brainstorm the impact the company has internally and on the world, plus how employees play a part in it, starts with engaging in meaningful and unfiltered conversations. It is thus no false assumption to make that discussing purpose calls for Emotional inclusion.

Within the arena of mental health or Emotional wellness, making a positive impact on the lives of our employees is a purpose we should all be zeroing in on, the pull is greater than us either way. How we choose to cultivate a sense of connection with each other starts with making a personal commitment to being open, respectful, and understanding of each other's emotions and belief structures. It enables us to communicate and interact more efficiently with each other and reach sustainable end-line goals. In the aftermath of the pandemic, mental well-being at work is now more important than ever; vesting time in grasping how we are helping our employees is essential.

A few questions I invite organizations to ask themselves in this 'purpose pursuit' are:

- How are you changing lives for good within your organizations in a holistic, personalized, and sustainable way?
- How do you support your company's mental well-being vision and how do you help your employees find meaning in it?
- How do you choose to advocate workplace well-being to create significant ripples of change?

These are big questions and call for a deep dive into a subject matter that has been swept under the carpet for far too long. Yet if we are serious about the humanization of our workplace, we simply cannot bypass the realm of our employees' well-being and the newfound purpose we choose to vest in the matter.

The World Health Organization is very adamant in that we can and should protect mental health within our organizations. It is both our duty as employers and a right for employees to feel safe and cared for at work. It cites that almost 60 per cent of the world population is in work[101]. Protecting and promoting mental health at work is what will create and enable workplace change. If we do not instil a sense of confidence and purpose, we will incapacitate the realm of Emotional inclusion. And we will, by definition, put the brakes on driving the workplace of the future in a way that puts our people at the centre of our organizational growth. How we inspire employees to give their best must go beyond the antiquated ways we have been following thus far at work. It starts with the acceptance of a human-centred mindset and moving forward with tangible, value-driven action.

Catalysing Change

As we have discussed in this chapter, solidarity, prevention, kindness, flexibility, vulnerability, empathy, compassion, listening, trust, confidentiality, and purpose all catalyse Emotional inclusion through a sense of authentic belonging. It is a new model of work that calls for a personalized human work culture that is in accordance with companies' DNA. The world's best organizations, those which think outside the box and holistically are the ones that embrace the concept of humanization of work.

---

[101] 'Emotional wellness at work', World Health Organization, (2022, September 28), retrieved February 25, 2023, https://www.who.int/news-room/fact-sheets/detail/mental-health-at-work.

A recent article penned by Deloitte estimated the cost of neglecting well-being at a whopping $20 million in opportunity loss for every 10,000 workers[102] due to low well-being's drain on performance. Deloitte found that 'improving worker well-being' was a top outcome that employees wanted from work transformation efforts. The issue is there is still a huge, persistent disconnect between employers and employees. 65 per cent of Chief Human Resources Officers say their organization cares about employee well-being, while only 24 per cent of their employees say the same, the report adds.

We need there to be more transparency in corporate communication if we want to move away from our outmoded workplace landscape. If we are not more human, open, and caring in our approach to listen and take action on what our employees are telling us, there will be no moving forward. Making well-being tied to Emotional inclusion a part of daily work life is vital. The result is nothing less than a cultural transformation toward a more human workplace. Emotional inclusion cannot exist without action. In the next chapter, we break down exactly why this is.

---

[102] Thorne, S., & Codd, E. (2022, October 18) 'Menopause And Work: Ending the Stigma', *Forbes*, retrieved February 24, 2023, https://www.forbes.com/sites/deloitte/2022/10/18/menopause-and-work-ending-the-stigma/?sh=7fef49a41eee.

Key Takeaways

- There is an awakening of the need for Emotional inclusion in the workplace, but it is staggered and unintegrated, as there is no roadmap for employers and employees. What exactly must we do to be emotionally inclusive? To help more people get on board, we need to spell out the behaviours that have to take place.

- Solidarity is one integral component. While we all have unique and individual experiences, solidarity is the glue that binds individuals in an organization. It goes beyond promoting connections towards the company DNA and into authentic, purposeful, shared actions. Solidarity occurs when employees unite around a value that strikes a chord with them—whether that's mental health or Emotional wellness at work, sustainability, organizational values, or more—and find a joint meaning, as a collective, in not just the betterment of their lives but also the betterment of the corporate culture.

- Prevention is needed in our efforts to humanize the work landscape. We must be cautious of 'false assessments'— which are barriers that prevent connection between people—in how we interact with each other and how we engage in active, unfiltered communication. Leaders need to clearly map out what a toxic workplace might look like so that we zero in on prevention and provide action-driven policies and pillars that back up mental health efforts.

- If people truly are at the heart of every business, then fostering kindness brings the 'heart' back into doing business. It stretches beyond compliments to the entire spectrum of showing concern for others. While the move to online work has removed the chance of serendipitous opportunities to show kindness in person, we can harness technologies to replace these moments, such as through virtual meetings and online chats. We are social creatures who thrive on affirmation. Organizations that know how to foster this are arguably more successful because an employee who feels recognized and validated will always pay it back.

- Flexibility is the ability to adapt, and when it comes to the workplace of the future, we are called to forgo all archaic practices to make room for change. Employees are now demanding a new model of work: flexible schedules, flexible workstations, and more such benefits to greater satisfaction, retention, engagement, and loyalty. We live in a rapidly changing world and are thus called to practice flexibility in questioning the status quo.

- Encouraging vulnerability in the workplace is unavoidable. Because people, especially leaders, are so afraid of being judged and rejected for showing their struggles, they spend most of their lives pretending they have it all together. Great power resides in leaders acting on their vulnerability to showcase their fallibility. This mask is intensely depleting to maintain. In revealing to others that we cannot fragment our lives into neat boxes for the sake of workplace norms, we are doing ourselves and others a moral and ethical favour. Vulnerability does not mean fragility; rather, it is about being real. What this does is spearhead meaningful, authentic connections where employees feel more fulfilled and safer, leading to enhanced feelings of self-worth, increased creativity and innovation, deeper workplace relationships, and better quality work output.

- Empathy allows us to connect with colleagues in a deeper way than superficial chitchat or dry one-on-ones. Empathy is our emotionally inclusive radar; it allows us to think of strategies to put others at ease. Having experienced it ourselves, we understand the pain of someone going through loss, sickness, heartbreak, even if the stigma prevents them from sharing more. And empathy is the first step toward compassion, and employees are quick to discern non-compassionate employers that do not have their back. Instead of rerouting Emotional conversations back to workplace demands, leaders should hold space for employees to speak up when they are struggling. And the employee served with such compassion will surely pay it back a hundredfold. In this vein, taking time to listen to a colleague or employee can be tremendously powerful if we want people to speak up in our organizations.

- Two years on from the remote work wave, we are still having to evaluate how to incorporate trust as a foundational pillar within our companies. Trust breeds workplace engagement, stronger morals, and a sense of belonging. Meanwhile, poor trust means employees are less likely to recommend their workplace, leading to smaller talent pools, and lower productivity, as the perception of low trust hurts workers' daily effort.

- To obtain trust, confidentiality is needed: the fundamental problem today is that there is profound employee distrust of organizations. Confidential support and treatment for mental health should be provided to all employees as part of their overall health benefits package.

- Purpose is a by-product of Emotional inclusion and requires being responsive to the Emotional aspirations of employees. Employers who fail to meet this need should be prepared to lose talent to other companies that will. How much time do companies vest in authentically engaging with their employees to understand what would make their jobs more meaningful? In the aftermath of the pandemic, mental well-being at work is now more important than ever; vesting time in grasping how we are helping our employees is essential.
- Emotional inclusion is a new model of work that calls for us to embrace the concept of humanization of work. If we are not more human, open, and caring in our approach to listen and take action on what our employees are telling us, there will be no moving forward.

Part VI

Inclusion is an Action

'Each human being, however small or weak, has something to bring to humanity. As we start to really get to know others, as we begin to listen to each other's stories, things begin to change. We begin the movement from exclusion to inclusion, from fear to trust, from closedness to openness, from judgment and prejudice to forgiveness and understanding. It is a movement of the heart.'[103]

—JEAN VANIER

Inclusion is a universal human right.

The Cambridge Business English Dictionary puts it as 'the act of allowing many different types of people to do something and treating them fairly and equally'[104]. I will humbly allow myself to fine tune this definition by stating that the objective of inclusion is to welcome, listen, accept, and support all people regardless of race, gender, disability, and medical or other needs.

---

[103] Vanier, Jean (1998) *Becoming Human*, Paulist Press.

[104] 'Inclusion', Cambridge Dictionary, retrieved February 28, 2023, https://dictionary.cambridge.org/us/dictionary/english/inclusion.

It is providing the same access and opportunities for all whilst getting rid of stigma, unfairness, judgement, and intolerance. Bain & Company's definition is one that I value as well, as it gives it an additional complementary spin. They state, 'We define inclusion as the feeling of belonging in your organization and team, feeling treated with dignity as an individual, and feeling encouraged to fully participate and bring your uniqueness to work every day'.[105]

Overcoming the boundaries of Emotional inclusion in the workplace takes more than merely speaking about it. Challenging stereotypes and allowing our employees to feel comfortable in bringing their full selves to work calls for laser-focused action. If we are to look at a means to a bigger end, we need to be clear on the fact that transparent accountability sets the culture. In shaping a human-centric workspace, we need an organizational culture where everybody—up and down the hierarchy—is willing to take responsibility for their actions. Workplace culture needs to encourage and empower all members to take risks in owning both the power and the consequences of what they do. Yet, as we all know, this is easier said than done.

Making the Case for Emotional Inclusion

Neuroscientist Matthew Lieberman's research suggests that the human brain is constantly scanning and assessing the environment for possible signs of rejection and social exclusion[106]. This is to keep us alive and out of harm's way. Lieberman and his lab at

[105] Coffman, J., Bax, B., Noether, A., & Blair, B., 'The Fabric of Belonging: How to Weave an Inclusive Culture', Bain & Company, retrieved February 26, 2023, from https://www.bain.com/insights/the-fabric-of-belonging-how-to-weave-an-inclusive-culture/?gclid=Cj0KCQiA4OybBhCzARIsAIcfn9 kwcCvBGuBp-P7ACJX-cTMJlE-PjDjv9Yzrwkm1RLT1uFFYL0nehGEa-AlujEALw_wcB.

[106] Lieberman, M. D. (2015) *Social: Why Our Brains are Wired to Connect*, Oxford University Press.

the University of California, Los Angeles found that our brains react to social pain and pleasure in much the same way as they do to physical pain and pleasure. As human beings, we are wired to self-preserve, to choose pleasure over pain and comfort over fear. Being emotionally exclusive will have the same effect: it will catalyse fear, mistrust, estrangement, and separation.

How this trickles down to our workplaces has a profound snowball effect on the macroeconomy. Even before the pandemic, the World Health Organization estimated that depression affects about 300 million people worldwide[107] and yet the irony of it is, post-pandemic, organizations globally are literally still scrambling in this arena. The silver lining of COVID-19 was that it brought a big mirror in front of humanity by effectively bringing mental health challenges to everyone's doorstep. And we are still very much in the eye of the storm, as we grapple with issues such as burnout, anxiety, depression, loneliness, grief, stress, and fear. According to research from Diversity Council Australia, work has a negative impact on the mental health of one in three workers, and those working in non-inclusive teams are seven times less likely to report their workplace as safe and supportive for those with poor mental health[108]. It argues that 'inclusion—whether in teams, leaders, or the organizational culture—is linked to better mental health at work'.

---

[107] 'Depression and Other Common Mental Disorders Global Health Estimates [Report]', World Health Organization, retrieved February 26, 2023, http://apps.who.int/iris/bitstream/handle/10665/254610/WHO-MSD-MER-2017.2-eng.pdf;jsessionid=5F11942488365D48586C1B366EABCC3C?sequence=1. 2017.

[108] 'Mapping the State of Inclusion and Mental Health in the Australian Workforce', Diversity Council Australia, retrieved February 26, 2023, https://www.dca.org.au/research/project/mapping-state-inclusion-and-mental-health-australian-workforce?utm_source=DCA+Updates&utm_campaign=55f078a1f2-INDEX_MH_2022_05_19&utm_medium=email&utm_term=0_bcbe24e7e8-55f078a1f2-81340371.

While we are starting to see positive changes to influence well-being inclusion in companies, few are still making it a talent and risk strategy priority. Why? Well, because it calls for them to take an honest look at how well their internal wellness barometer is doing. It also takes courage from the top to actively tackle a subject matter that so many are still shying away from due to the stigma. Lack of awareness in the mental well-being arena is another reason; and so, the task of putting together a robust support system in place can be daunting. Confusion on where to start and how to obtain the most effective return on investment is, let us face it, widely rampant.

And then there is another problem to take into consideration: the shortage of professionally trained people such as psychiatrists and counsellors. According to data from the World Health Organization, the number of psychologists, psychiatrists, social workers, and nurses in the mental health sector in the majority of nations in 2017 was less than ten each per 100,000 individuals[109]. Johnson & Johnson even claims some countries have no mental health professionals at all[110]. 'Geographic maldistribution adds to the difficulties with access to care', writes Allan Tasman, editor of the publication *Psychiatric Times*, in an editorial succinctly titled 'Too Few Psychiatrists for Too Many'[111]. 'In China, for example', Tasman explains, 'about 80 per cent of psychiatrists are in urban

---

[109] 'Mental health workers – Data by country', World Health Organization (WHO), retrieved February 26, 2023, https://apps.who.int/gho/data/view.main.HWF11v.

[110] Derrow, P. (2021, October 7) 'How Johnson & Johnson Supports Future Mental Health Leaders', Johnson & Johnson, retrieved February 26, 2023, https://www.jnj.com/personal-stories/%20how-johnson-johnson-is-supporting-future-mental-health-leaders.

[111] Tasman, A. (2015, April 16) 'Too Few Psychiatrists for Too Many', *Psychiatric Times*, retrieved February 26, 2023, https://www.psychiatrictimes.com/view/too-few-psychiatrists-too-many.

areas, while about 80 per cent of the population still lives in the countryside.'

As the data highlights so clearly, the glaring lack of accredited professionals shows that the lack of medical professionals is a limiting factor in workers' access to mental healthcare. As we have covered, the need for Emotional inclusion in our companies is pressing, and other avenues to tackle the matter could, for instance, be found in further promoting accelerated organizational psychology degrees. Organizational psychology, also called occupational psychology, tackles the theme of people in the workplace. It examines behaviours and workplace dynamics to improve organizational undercurrents for the better. It is also common practice for certain universities to allow students to tackle specific subjects within organizational psychology. These include human resources, culture and diversity, leadership, negotiation and conflict management, and so on[112].

Whilst universities classically require a bachelor's degree in psychology to pursue this credential, some admissions offices, depending on the school, will sometimes be inclined to take into account other criteria. These typically include professional experience, relevant undergraduate test scores, or training within the given arena. A Masters degree in organizational psychology takes, on an average, two to two-and-a-half years to complete. There is no doubt in my mind that companies seeking to instil Emotional inclusion in their companies could either offer this degree to their employees or make it a prerequisite for their Human Resources managers, leaders, or DEI officers. Could we make this approach the new emotionally inclusive way forward? As a leader, I would take the opportunity in a heartbeat. As a matter of fact, even if not yet offered within my company, getting

---

[112] 'FAQ: What can you do with an organizational psychology master's?' Indeed, retrieved March 16, 2023, https://www.indeed.com/career-advice/career-development/organizational-psychology-masters. (2022, June 25)

an organizational psychology degree is on my own personal agenda already. The realm of the human is a vast and complex one to which none of us have all the answers. Yet what we do know is that the psychological cost of exclusion is costing us a great deal more.

A Voice for Real Change

Bringing back the legitimacy of Emotional inclusion at work to create a sense of belonging remains a priority. For this we want more dialogues, not monologues. 'Perspective-taking is a life skill, not just a workplace one', write inclusion consultants Selena Rezvani and Stacey Gordon in a *Harvard Business Review* article[113]. 'Companies that prioritize inclusion will emerge from crisis stronger, and stories are one major vehicle to help them get there.'

No doubt that stories have the power to inspire, strengthen, and heal. They have the power to connect people and harbour trust. They help shape how we think about our lives, but they also inspire others to learn how they can be their best selves. It is a safe assumption then to say that storytelling programmes in the workplace are altogether an effective tool to engage in conversations on mental health or Emotional wellness. And truth be told, we all have a story to tell.

How can organizations leverage and amplify storytelling, such as inclusion videos, or mental health media campaigns that feature their employees? Larger companies are mainly the ones doing so for now (and I do not buy into the fact that it is because they have greater resources): Shell, Dell, HSBC, Expedia, Deloitte, and Johnson & Johnson, to name a few. JanSport, the American backpack brand, particularly caught my attention

---

[113] Rezvani, S., & Gordon, S.A. (2021, November 1) 'How Sharing Our Stories Builds Inclusion', *Harvard Business Review*, retrieved February 26, 2023, https://hbr.org/2021/11/how-sharing-our-stories-builds-inclusion.

with their #LightenTheLoad social media campaign, which was created to drive open conversations among Gen Z around mental health or Emotional wellness. Citing findings from Pew Research that seven out of ten young people say their mental health is weighing them down, JanSport was on a mission to connect young people with the tools to unpack mental health, such as access to therapists and links to online resources and initiatives. Their message? 'If you're not sharing it, you're carrying it. If something's weighing you down, let it out with #ShareItChallenge to help lighten the load.' I find the tagline brilliant and on point. Not being able to speak up at work is truly like carrying a secret, heavy, Emotional load.

What JanSport is doing here is proving that its company values Emotional inclusion and belonging by uncovering and amplifying a variety of voices. They are proving, through action, that there is real strength in sharing, to make a real impact in changing how a generation is navigating the effects of the pandemic and of the stresses of life altogether. They are taking the lead by sharing stories told by real people, tackling topics like depression and anxiety, family conflict, and coming to terms with identity. What they are essentially doing is providing a platform for the voices of young people—particularly those of Gen Z, the generation most likely to report mental health concerns[114]—and so enhancing the group's ability to reduce stigma around mental health or Emotional wellness in future workplaces.

One might question how much JanSport's campaign is sheer marketing versus truly wanting to make a difference. For the sceptics out there, sure, this might be a debatable topic, yet the #LightenTheLoad campaign worked because JanSport was clear on its Gen Z target audience and it allowed them to deep dive

---

[114] Bethune, S. (2019, January 1) 'Gen Z more likely to report mental health concerns', American Psychological Association, retrieved February 26, 2023, https://www.apa.org/monitor/2019/01/gen-z.

into how they could be of value and support by listening to the priorities and concerns of this group. What this does in return is spearhead engagement and visibility and kickstart meaningful conversations. I like to think of this as positive, even as we judge the authenticity of such campaigns with skepticism.

In another example, there is Canadian telecommunications company, Bell, whose brand identity is tied to open discussions on mental health in the nation. For more than a decade, its 'Bell Let's Talk' campaign has helped reduce stigma and increase conversations surrounding mental illness through not only the hundreds of millions it has donated to fund mental health research and access, but also its annual 'Let's Talk Day', a social media campaign meant to drive chatter around its hashtag, #BellLetsTalk, which is meant to catalyse conversations on mental health in the community.

At my organization, Emotional inclusion® in the Workplace, we did a #MyMentalHealthPledge media campaign timed with Mental Health Awareness Month (found on our website should you wish to take a look at it) in which we rallied global leaders to bravely speak up on what their commitment is to the realm of Emotional wellness within their specific organizations and arenas. Why we chose leaders to partake in the campaign is because we know that real change starts from the top. In order to encourage other organizations to take the lead on Emotional wellness, we found it sound to help pave the way by sharing encouraging and convincing messages from established leaders. Too many are still hiding out on the matter of Emotional wellness: speaking about it behind closed doors is to some degree acceptable, but God forbid, being asked to speak publicly on the matter is a whole other kettle of fish.

Leaders, managers, and peers all have a responsibility and an instrumental part to play in driving a culture of increased Emotional inclusion in the workplace. Harbouring conscious

Emotional inclusion means being transparent towards our commitments to minimize mental health or Emotional wellness bias and walk our talk. It is also inviting companies to actively listen to make actionable change. Because, let us face it, educating ourselves is the only way to cleanse the organizational environment of bias and is the way to make workplace adjustments. And I believe all companies should have a passion for courageous and brave Emotional inclusion!

The Road Ahead

As the World Health Organization writes, 'There is no health without mental health'.[115] Organizations can only change the lives of their employees for the better through action. And what leaders can do as a group for mental health or Emotional wellness and Emotional inclusion in the workplace is undeniably where their power resides.

Companies have a moral obligation to cultivate an emotionally inclusive, human-centric culture for their employees, shareholders, and communities. And the reality is that this moral responsibility needs to still be spelt out, as it is still somehow very misunderstood and confusing for most. Addressing the core fundamental ethical issues such as Emotional safety, dignity, and equality needs a framework. You might now be wondering what this might look like.

I would argue, as I have several times in this book, that Emotional inclusion should be part of companies' DEI agendas—at the genesis, I coined the term 'Emotional inclusion' when I realized that DEI platforms spoke of all types of inclusion, but not of inclusion when it came to the

---

[115] 'Health and Well-Being', World Health Organization, retrieved February 27, 2023, https://www.who.int/data/gho/data/major-themes/health-and-well-being.

Emotional realm. And yet, would not you say that it is perhaps the one commonality that ties us together as a species? It is the missing piece of the puzzle of the human workplace. Many organizations are adopting agile working and communication programmes when it comes to inclusion; however, few are the ones who focus on what workplace Emotional guidance can look like, with information on Emotional symptoms, ways to alleviate them at work, leading practices in providing support, and offering resources for leaders, such as how to pinpoint and tackle their team's Emotional triggers.

The first port of call is revaluating the lives of our employees at work and being honest about it. Are they genuinely happy with the organizational culture they spend most of their waking hours being a part of? Do they have a general sense of belonging and purpose that drives their Emotional wellness? Do they feel cared for on a mental health benefit scale? Do they feel safe speaking up? Do they feel the company is genuinely putting their well-being at the centre of their agendas?

Employers—ready or not—will need to help meet this need or be prepared to lose talent to companies that will. The benefits of getting individual purpose right are substantial, self-reinforcing, and extend not only to the well-being of employees but also to the company's performance. I propose the term *conscious Emotional inclusion* because it takes developing our awareness and being candid on what needs to change if we wish to sustainably shape a more humane workplace of the future. As former captain of the US women's national soccer team Julie Floudy puts it, 'It's our responsibility to show our communities the value of all people, to celebrate different, and to take a stand for acceptance and inclusion'.[116]

---

[116] Foudy, J. (2014, June 5) 'I'm Taking a Stand Because There Is Value in All People', *HuffPost*, retrieved February 27, 2023, https://www.huffpost.com/entry/im-taking-a-stand-because_b_5452618.

Where there is a lack of Emotional inclusion, we must address the issue from the top and invest in educating our leaders so that they can help shape the company culture in such a way that employees feel heard and that they are treated fairly and humanly. Another point would be to create solid communication channels, not just in storytelling or media campaigns for the world to see, but internally for employees to feel secure in their sharing. Learning to receive and implement feedback is also crucial. How much we choose to listen to what our employees have to say and how quickly and efficiently we then act upon what is said largely contributes to the notion of accountability. So too does providing solutions that answer their needs—it means a great deal in the trust-building process. Employees quietly take note of what gets done, or not done, as it is unfortunately often the case.

Aside from Emotional inclusion, which I discuss in this book, there are other forms of inclusion that complement the advice I have been giving companies looking to improve workplace inclusiveness. I find these three the most relevant:

1. Work team inclusion encompasses healthy job satisfaction, where employees feel included in a joint purpose set by the organization. They share a sense of common belonging, and they know that their story matters and is heard, devoid of judgement.

2. Leadership inclusion sees leaders act swiftly when it comes to answering the needs voiced by their employees. This, in turn, catalyses their ability to be seen as leaders who truly care and can be depended on. By ensuring accountability toward employees, leaders weave within their teams trust, security, receptiveness, and honest communication, which all contribute to enhance productivity.

3. Organizational inclusion encourages all employees to fully participate and bring their uniqueness to work every day.

It rallies the workforce in a way in which each individual feels a sense of purpose, and that their uniqueness is valued by the organization.

Beyond these, there is also the simple act of accepting and embracing of our employees for who they are, and I realize that you might have a harder time with this one, but hear me out. Regardless of their background, beliefs, personal orientations, or even their personality, workers need to know that their workplace is a judgement-free one in order to perform at their best. The strong link between inclusion and performance is undeniable. According to Deloitte, inclusive workplaces are twice as likely to meet or exceed financial goals and six times more likely to be innovative[117]. The experts at management consultants Bain & Company say that those who feel 'fully included' are *much* more likely to recommend others to work at their organization[118]. And those who feel able to bring their whole selves to work are 42 per cent less likely to leave within a year for another opportunity, write DEI experts Laura Sherbin and Ripa Rashid[119]. At the core, the higher the level of inclusion, the higher the level of well-being and engagement among employees, which can lead to better business results.

---

[117] 'New Deloitte Research Identifies Keys to Creating Fair and Inclusive Organizations', PR *Newswire*, retrieved February 27, 2023, https://www. prnewswire.com/news-releases/new-deloitte-research-identifies-keys-to-creating-fair-and-inclusive-organizations-300455164.html. (2017, May 10).

[118] Coffman, J., Bax, B., Noether, A., & Blair, B. 'The Fabric of Belonging: How to Weave an Inclusive Culture', Bain & Company, retrieved February 26, 2023, https://www.bain.com/insights/the-fabric-of-belonging-how-to-weave-an-inclusive-culture/?gclid=Cj0KCQiA4OybBhCzARIsAIcfn9 kwcCvBGuBp-P7ACJX-cTMJlE-PjDjv9Yzrwkm1RLT1uFFYL0nehGEa-AlujEALw_wcB.

[119] Sherbin, L., & Rashid, R. (2017, February 1) 'Diversity Doesn't Stick Without Inclusion', *Harvard Business Review*, retrieved February 27, 2023, https://hbr.org/2017/02/diversity-doesnt-stick-without-inclusion.

It bears emphasizing that the arrival of Emotional inclusion in workplaces does not herald the sacrificing of business needs in favour of employee ones. Rather, an Emotionally inclusive, human-centric culture values learning. When an employee's work needs improvement, they need to be provided with the opportunity to grow and change. We can still hold people accountable for the work they do and be kind. How we choose to respond to their humanity measures the depth of our Emotional inclusiveness.

If—in the words of diversity consultant Verna Myers— 'diversity is being invited to the party; inclusion is being asked to dance',[120] then let us all dance the hell away to the tune of destigmatizing mental health. And if you deem yourself a bad dancer, then face your fear and join right in. 'Fears are nothing more than a state of mind', goes the quote from American self-help author Napoleon Hill. So, fear not, because the psychological impacts of exclusion are far worse.

If inclusion is how we are made to feel when being asked to dance, then Emotional inclusion is how well we are made to feel when we reach the office; how emotionally connected we are to our colleagues, to our leaders at work, and to the greater organizational values and purpose. It is the knowing and the feeling that we 'belong' in a caring, judgement-free, and safe environment, where we know we can show up as our full selves at work. It is the ability to trust the companies' Emotional wellness infrastructure and the willingness to break down mental health and Emotional barriers. Weaving an emotionally inclusive culture takes time, patience, and a solid plan of action at an infrastructural level. There is no quick fix. Instead, a whole lot of testing and trying is needed for there to be sustainable and authentic change.

---

[120] Cho, J.H. (2016, May 25) 'Diversity is being invited to the party and asked to dance', Cleveland.com, retrieved February 27, 2023, https://www.cleveland.com/business/2016/05/diversity_is_being_invited_to.html.

Key Takeaways

- Emotional inclusion programmes should be part of every company's global Diversity, Equity, and Inclusion (DEI) agendas, focusing on what workplace Emotional guidance can look like, with information on Emotional symptoms, ways to alleviate them at work, leading practices in providing support, and resources for leaders, such as how to pinpoint and tackle their team's Emotional triggers.
- Combined with lack of awareness on the mental well-being arena, the task of putting together a robust support system can be daunting. There is confusion around how to obtain the most effective return on investment, as well as a shortage of professionals such as psychiatrists and counsellors. How can we take steps to tackle this through piloting new, more efficient models of learning and training?
- Allowing employees to feel comfortable in bringing their full selves to work calls for organizations to be transparent and accountable towards their commitments to minimize mental health bias. Educating ourselves is one way to break the bias and mark workplace adjustments in how we deal with mental health issues. Another is solid communication channels, both internally for employees, as well as externally to the public through media campaigns. Though some may regard such marketing initiatives with skepticism, these are still positive steps to listen to staff and customers and act quickly and efficiently upon what is said.
- While we are starting to see more awareness from corporates around well-being inclusion, few are making

it a priority because it calls for them to take an honest look at how well their people truly are. It takes courage from the top to evaluate if employees feel cared for from a mental health perspective, feel safe about speaking up, and feel that the company is genuinely putting their well-being at the centrefold of agendas. Where there is a lack of Emotional inclusion, we must invest in educating leaders so that they can help shape the company culture. If we wish to sustainably shape a more humane workplace of the future, we must be candid about what needs to change.

- The silver lining of COVID-19 was that it brought a big mirror in front of humanity, bringing mental health challenges to everyone's door. We are still very much in the eye of the storm, as the world continues to grapple with burnout, anxiety, depression, loneliness, grief, stress, and fear. There is no better moment for an Emotional inclusion movement than now.

- Emotional inclusion is how well we are made to feel when we reach the office. There is no quick fix to create an Emotionally inclusive culture. It will take time and trial, but it is a worthy, meaningful, and much needed endeavour for humanity.

Part VII

A New, Emotionally-Inclusive Era

'The secret of change is to focus all of your energy not on fighting the old, but on building the new.'[121]

—DAN MILLMAN

It was important for me to conclude this book with a chapter that echoes positive expectation for what lies ahead within the realm of Emotional inclusion. As the workplace mental health or Emotional wellness landscape begins to change, so should we change with it, too.

Emotional inclusion calls for collective and individual action when it comes to our humanness at work. After all, the strength of an organization stems from each employee. Exploring other mental territories summons us to move forward together in knowing that the new workplace norm is closer to actualization than we think it is. The archaic robotic organizational ways no longer work and are not worth further dwelling upon. Instead,

---

[121] Millman, Dan (2006) *Way of the Peaceful Warrior: A Book That Changes Lives*, H J Kramer.

moving onwards and forward is where we are at today. The awareness of this, I like to think, is half the battle.

The Case for Emotional Inclusion

We have covered what the new organizational platform should look like, tracing it back historically, and shedding light on the mind-body conundrum. We have outlined the dangerous trap of stigma and the price we have paid for our ignorance. We have heard stories from leaders and individuals alike, who have shared their insights and challenges amidst their Emotional inclusion-starved workplaces, and what they have learnt from it. We have mapped out the top themes of humanizing the workplace and how to put them to practice. And finally, we have examined the fact that inclusion is an action, making for Emotional inclusion, a coined term that focuses on instilling key organizational pillars that embrace each other's Emotional realm, and thus, each other's humanity.

In the aftermath of COVID, our world has changed, we all have changed, and it has led even the best of companies to question what has gotten them to be 'the best' in the first place. We all know the answer to this at this stage. The focus on employees and caring for their well-being has become a topic no one can escape. Or let me rephrase this: Emotional inclusion has become a topic that no one can escape. Refocusing our values, our mission, and our vision for our workforce is now at the front of mind in the drive to increase wholesome profitability. Committing to new thinking is emerging as the only way forward, but framing it in a laser-focused, sustainable way is not coming across as easy to do, as evidenced in previous chapters. This post-COVID heightened awareness of mental wellness is leading us to not just shed light on the importance of Emotional inclusion in our workforce today, but also to micro-analyse how this is going to take shape in practice. Beyond ending this book on a hopeful note, the purpose of this final chapter is to give you an even more concrete idea of how Emotional inclusion is being implemented today and hopefully encourage you to trust the process as you go about marking the steps towards building an emotionally inclusive culture of your own.

Lessons in Experience

When leaders and managers walk their talk in advocating Emotional inclusion and raise awareness on the dire need to bring humanity back at the centre of their business agendas, greater acknowledgment arises in how much the workplace has failed to address the Emotional wellness of its employees up until now. The dialogue is deepened and the stigma that lies behind it is weakened. This moment in time is shedding light on the need for more resources and more tangible action. Studies are now specifically showcasing that more leaders and organizations alike are taking charge as they add up the numbers and realize that the impact on the Emotional welfare of people will likely worsen if not seriously tackled.

The World Economic Forum has, for example, revealed that Emotional unwellness globally accounted for $2.5 trillion in productivity loss, absences, and turnover[122]. In response to the issue, a recent survey found that over six in ten human resource leaders say that mental health and well-being is their top priority[123]. Scaling up mental health services is now becoming the centre of

[122] McCain, K., & Manktelow, A. (2021, January 25) '6 global employers on how to improve workplace mental health', The World Economic Forum, retrieved March 16, 2023, https://www.weforum.org/agenda/2021/01/6-global-employers-on-how-to-improve-workplace-mental-health/.

[123] 'How will the HR industry look in 2023? The results are in!' Natural HR, retrieved March 16, 2023, https://www.naturalhr.com/2023/02/06/hr-industry-2023-research-results-are-in/. (2023, February 6).

focus, and value-based leadership[124], one that takes into account the Emotional welfare of our people, is becoming an inescapable new status quo. Providing credibility and thoughtful leadership is where it is all at.

We are starting to see the need move in the right direction in the common understanding that Emotional inclusion is not an organizational risk per se, but rather a necessity toward fighting the already existent Emotional unwellness damage. That unless leaders and companies alike invest time and resources in Emotional inclusion, the workplace will be, if anything, an extremely isolating place for their employees. Mental health issues will represent the biggest productivity disruptor in the workplace if no drive for action is taken. Accountability here is key, yet this accountability must be healthy for both the leader and its employees.

A leader's responsibility, if I may clarify in a slight aparté, is to first make sure that they are emotionally healthy themselves so that they may lead successfully. Secondly, their role is to, as we have already ironed out, create an emotionally inclusive culture that is invested in employee mental health or Emotional wellness by providing the adequate pillars and resources.

When interviewing former Twitter Asia Pacific vice president Maya Hari on my Emotional inclusion podcast, she shared how the tech company invested in an in-house clinical psychologist to lead global employee wellness. This clinical psychologist acts as the subject matter expert and the leader of wellness programmes, thereby leading employee Emotional wellness on a few different fronts: resiliency programmes for stress or anxiety relief or any major life challenge that someone might be experiencing, financial well-being programmes, and a healthy diet and lifestyle

---

[124] Locke, A. (2022, July 14) 'Values-Based Leadership Supports Well-Being and Mental Health', University of Utah Health, retrieved March 16, 2023, https://uofuhealth.utah.edu/notes/2022/07/values-based-leadership-supports-well-being-and-mental-health.

in general. Companies like Johnson & Johnson have also, for example, instilled Employee Assistance Programmes that provide free psychological consultation for employees and their families because they too look at Emotional inclusion on a holistic front. Employee Assistance Programs fit particularly well into what Emotional inclusion in the workforce promotes and acts upon, which is to provide free counselling services and follow-up services to employees experiencing either personal or work-related issues that affect their health and Emotional well-being—such as stress, anxiety, burnout, family problems, grief, psychological disorders, substance abuse, etc. Counsellors and psychologists work in a consultative capacity with managers and/or human resources to tackle employee and organizational challenges and needs. It suffices to say that this work is highly preventative in workplace emergency response situations.

Both Twitter and J&J also invest in mental health 'diplomats' or 'champions' by training employees as first respondents, to form an extension of the Emotional wellness programmes they have in place.

There are, of course, a host of other companies that have put together measures with the aim to create a more Emotionally inclusive workplace. Shell is one, and its DEI head Lyn Lee splits the organization's efforts in four categories. The first is *self-care,* introduced in the form of toolkits for self-based learning, with modules such as resilience, where employees can learn to take care of themselves. They notably support this with a well-being allowance, which employees can use to take tangible action in caring for themselves in any way they see fit. The second pillar concentrates around *volunteer capability building* for staff who want to be wellness ambassadors and help colleagues who feel that they have no one to turn to. If an employee has been noticeably looking unwell or been missing from work, the idea is to check in with said person and ask if he or she is all right. They are not Emotional wellness experts per se, but they help signpost or troubleshoot, if you will, any signs of mental ill-health and act as a 'second layer of defence'. Toolkits are provided for the ambassadors.

The third pillar is their *Employee Assistance Programme*, where employees get access to short-term counselling, therapy, or receive some confidential psychological assessment. The fourth pillar stands for *specialists*, where employees can go to doctors to receive a free consultation, diagnosis, treatment, and long-term management where necessary. This is exactly what is missing in so many companies today, and what I advocate for: providing professional, confidential, robust mental health or Emotional wellness support to walk with employees through the vicissitudes of life.

To the Future and Beyond

Companies at large are becoming more emotionally connected and are slowly but surely taking out the prejudicial, stigma-ridden component of the term 'emotional'. To put it simply, the word 'emotional' is no longer being perceived as a bad word. It is about being human-centric and talking about productivity from a human-centred point of view.

Emotional inclusion is being moulded into the new workforce norm, and its impetus lies in looking at how we can get the best of our employees and how they can perform at their best. As previously outlined, the pull is greater than us at this stage, and the organizations of the future who do not include Emotional inclusion at the nucleus of their modus operandi will be left behind.

Neglecting to look at it seriously or downplaying the Emotional burden that employees are statistically experiencing is no longer an option. McKinsey found, in a study conducted across fifteen countries, that toxic workplace behaviour is the biggest prognosticator for burnout and turnover[125]. Emotional exclusion speaks for itself. Workplace ecosystems that incorporate Emotional inclusion are ones where the organization commits to promote belonging, value-based accountable leadership, supportive environments that are free from stigma, and humanistic, supportive growth. They provide action-based resources and platforms that employees can tap into so that they no longer have to suffer in silence, wondering if it is safe for them to speak up in fear of being penalized, being told they are not a high performer, or worse, losing their jobs.

Minimizing Emotional inclusion takes a toll on employees. We have covered the consequences and the negative impact this has on our people. Smaller companies might sometimes think that fostering Emotional inclusion is only possible for larger organizations that have the bandwidth, budget, and resources to instil it in their organizations. Yet this could not be further from the truth. Every company can promote it by opening up the discussion, inviting people to come talk about it, and directing their employees to free support platforms. The real-life experiences of leaders and employees that I have shared in this book serve as reminders that the way forward embraces Emotional inclusion. To recontextualize this, I thought I would add another story, one that showcases yet again the need for us to be wide awake when it comes to Emotional inclusion.

---

[125] Brassey, J., Coe, E., Dewhurst, M., Enomoto, K., Giarola, R., Herbig, B., & Jeffery, B. (2022, May 27) 'Addressing employee burnout: Are you solving the right problem?' McKinsey, retrieved March 16, 2023, https://www.mckinsey.com/mhi/our-insights/addressing-employee-burnout-are-you-solving-the-right-problem.

Marina Mathews, CEO & Founder, MM Communications

Growing up in a single-parent household, I had always promised myself that when I met my life partner, we would stay together forever. Sadly, this was not to be.

I became a first-time mother at the age of thirty-eight, and by the time I was forty-one, I had had my second child. I did not know it at the time but I was struggling with postnatal depression. That coincided with deciding that I would go back to work nine days after giving birth.

You are probably wondering why on earth a new mom would do that, but having started a new job only weeks after I found out I was pregnant, I wanted to prove to my boss that I was committed, capable, and competent.

It was during this dark period that my husband and I started having issues in our relationship: heated arguments, jealousy, and resentment built up. My husband was also not being able to cope with what I realized years later was the feeling of emasculation. It is not unusual, when your wife is the sole breadwinner and has a high income from her successful career while you feel like you are not contributing, especially when there is a new baby so reliant on its mother.

By the time my second-born was eight months old, and my eldest was three and a half years old, things had gotten worse. I was working crazy hours to keep up with the demands of a managing director role responsible for over twenty staff, while my husband was 'stuck' at home with the kids.

It was Valentine's Day and we had made no plans to celebrate, so I stayed back late at work as I had done most days. Our housekeeper had gone out for cooking classes earlier in the day, and as she arrived home, she heard screaming and shouting between my husband and our toddler in the bedroom. My husband yelled at her to go deal with our crying baby in the other room and what unfolded next was something no child should ever have to experience.

Triggered by our toddler's insistence on not taking his afternoon nap, my husband smacked his little backside and thighs until he was black and blue. He was so physically hurt that there were fingerprint bruises left all over him from the large hands of a 6'4" extremely athletic man.

A few days after the incident, and unbeknownst to me the entire time, as my husband was going above and beyond to hide any evidence, I eventually discovered the horrific bruising all over our toddler. Needless to say, this ended our relationship and I applied for ourt-ordered protection and domestic exclusion summons.

This made my husband go to another extreme. For weeks on end, I was receiving death threats and was the subject of so much Emotional abuse that I was at my wit's end as to how I could hide what I was going through at home from my staff as well as my boss, who was fortunately based overseas. Outside of work, I became extremely withdrawn and the polar opposite of my usual social self. I had no one to talk to, no HR team or person I could confide in within the company. I felt tremendous stigma and shame about what I was going through and fell into a deep depression.

Two months after the initial incident with our son, my husband physically attacked me. Ripping out about a third of the hair on my head and having had randomly cut off pieces of hair to escape his grip, this was more difficult to conceal from my colleagues at work. I resorted to wearing head scarves, getting a short haircut (which I have never had in my life), and wearing a ton of make-up and heavy clothing to conceal the bruising on my face and body. To this day, I am still surprised that no one noticed the degree of difference in my behaviour, or at least mentioned it. But perhaps they did.

Going through six months of hell, my work started to suffer. I was not the same person I was previously. All I could think about was how I had to watch my back in case he came for us, and I was spending a fortune on random short trips overseas with the kids just so I could have a sense of peace that he could not physically reach us, despite his continued psychological abuse using any means he could: phone calls, voice mails, text messages, and emails. I literally have hundreds of records.

> *Then came crunch time at work. I eventually shared with my boss that I was going through a difficult divorce, minus all the details, to which he seemed sympathetic. What eventually transpired was anything but sympathetic. All of a sudden, major business decisions were being made without my knowledge, unexpected visits to our office took place, and I was asked to report back on pretty much my daily duties. How could this happen when I had turned this business into a highly profitable outpost and had built an amazing team who were delivering excellent results is beyond me.*
>
> *After parting with the organization, which was presented to the team as a mutual decision (but was not), I eventually embarked on setting up my own business. This time it would be a place of kindness, a place where topics considered taboo were talked about openly, and a place where leadership made you feel safe. Today, I am extremely proud of the emotionally inclusive workplace environment I have created, and suffice to say, our team is thriving.*

Emotional inclusion calls upon companies to acknowledge the humanness of its employees, it calls for them to recognize that life sometimes gets messy, that no one is spared from it and that the Emotional realm of its workforce needs to be protected and cared for. Organizations, big and small, need to look into how the Emotional welfare of their employees is integrated into the very fabric of their workplace culture, and understand that it is a direct reflection of the value structure they withhold. What Emotional inclusion can and will do is breed a human unitedness in the organization that will serve it a hundredfold. In the next anecdote, Lucia Keser speaks about this further.

LUCIA KESER, COACHING THERAPIST

As a coaching therapist working with many entrepreneurs, CEOs, and employees, it strikes me that the feeling of unease and fear around the 'allowing of emotions' in the workplace is the same on both sides.

I see people struggling to conceal emotions at work and keeping as their main goal the avoidance, denial, and shielding of what they truly feel. They force themselves to be perceived as okay. Sadly, this never works and cannot ever work. The amount of energy and focus this 'disguise' absorbs is obviously noticeable through lower productivity and quality of work, which is exactly what they are trying to avoid.

A good example is a client of mine, a business owner with 120 staff. He went through a traumatic period of spiralling after the personal loss of two people close to him and denied himself the space to mourn properly out of fear that his employees would lose trust in his leadership. He kept focusing on not being perceived as weak or feeble. All his energy was sucked up by this role he played, and he became paralysed, unable to make decisions, as small as they may be. When we started working together, he strongly rejected words such as 'mental health' and 'burnout' and categorized them as things that mankind invented as an excuse for weakness. Unfortunately, I encounter this belief often in European management.

Focusing on awareness of his traumatized self was the first step in his healing. As we continued the journey to self-compassion, his views on being a man, a spouse, a father, and a business leader started to transform. Empathy through real listening became his priority and, needless to say, people around him started to notice the change. His fears about being vulnerable and showing up more fully dissipated, and he experienced more freedom when communicating. At the end of our work together, his company cooperated, and still does, with a platform of psychologists, available for all employees at any time and for any length of time. An even better practice is having an in-house trained psychologist, who equally understands the dynamics and DNA of the company, leading to the safest environment for all to thrive in.

Another example is of a New York client joining a prestigious consulting firm as a partner. After a long career of overachieving and overworking to compete with her male colleagues, she had finally landed her dream job. She felt on top of the world and knew that all the hard work had paid off.

The price she paid to focus entirely on her career was that she had covered up emotions with the rigid belief that being a woman is associated with weakness. She learned to act as a 'man' in the corporate environment, who she thought had to be emotionless and diehard. Initially, the role she played seemed to serve her well, as she was often complimented in the workplace for her fierce and strong behaviour.

And then, six months into the job, the masquerade was shattered. This is when I started working with her. Having ignored all the signs over the years, her body screamed out that it was enough. Notwithstanding her discipline and usual boundless energy, fatigue had put her flat out. Her body became her enemy.

From the moment she reported her medical issues to her boss, she was put to the side, excluded from meetings with the message that they wanted her to take the time to heal. Despite being on sick leave, her mailbox overflowed, and she received as many phone calls as she did when working. There was absolutely no attention nor any form of empathy, not even from her PA.

Now she had a double battle. On the one hand, she coped with the incomprehension, which brought high levels of fear, and on the other hand, her ill health. The combination of these brought her healing to a standstill and she had no other option than to prioritize her health. Fear evolved into anger and propelled her into new thinking: when she was healed, she would create an environment for herself and others where whatever happened, there would be a safety net of care. There was a big paradigm shift, a renewal of her identity, letting go of what she had become over the years: over-identified with a false idea of what success meant. It took her two years of loneliness and hardship to reinvent herself.

She now contently runs a small consulting firm, where all employees have equal say, as they are all partners. It is a safe place, where staff feel heard, are free to speak up, and where time off is respected.

Both examples show that getting help in navigating the workspace is essential in order to thrive. The taboo on expressing emotions when dealing with adverse situations in the workplace has not evolved much over the years. Big budgets are spent on innovative rewards and benefit schemes and seem to miss the core problem. When a person goes through emotionally triggering times, there is no quick fix, and no one solution fits all.

A person struggling with emotions will feel separated from the world. It seems to them that everyone is functioning, and they are the only ones struggling. The feeling that 'there is something wrong with me' isolates us and finding the way out might take too long to keep a job, let alone be efficient. It is a very lonely experience. Only through person-to-person connection in full compassion, seeing and hearing their suffering, can that isolation be broken. And that will be the first step in the healing process.

In a post COVID-19 world, and in the full swing of the virtual world and social media, I see many signs of disconnected people. People too scared to engage in 'real' relationships and preferring working from a shielded home base. The movement of Emotional inclusion in companies will be the right way forward to lower mental illness and enhance well-being on the work floor. It is a way forward for companies and humanity; by investing in people individually, we will gain collectively.

As psychologist Louis Cozolino puts it, 'Those who are nurtured best, survive best'.[126] The fact of the matter is that we all have to gain from emotionally inclusive and healthier workplaces.

---

[126] Cozolino, L. (2014) *The Neuroscience of Human Relationships: Attachment and the Developing Social Brain* (Second ed.), W.W. Norton.

Shifting gears from Emotional intelligence to a more action-driven, emotionally inclusive speed is where we have arrived at. And it is now well overdue that we put pedal to the metal. To walk our talk in how we care for the individuals we employ is no longer a nice-to-have but a dire necessity. Integrating sustainable mental health or Emotional wellness pillars that are tailored to each organization is paving the way to what being emotionally inclusive is all about. The transformation of moving forward from a thinking-based mentality to a proactive, emotionally inclusive practice is already happening at the workforce. The world has changed, and all of us have changed with it too. Call it the silver lining of the pandemic if you will, the mass awakening to Emotional inclusion has taken form, and it is revolutionizing the workplace like never before.

Key Takeaways

- While Emotional inclusion is lacking in many firms and a relatively new concept in most organizations, it is not all doom and gloom. The new normal at workplaces is closer to actualization than we think it is.
- As the workplace mental health or Emotional wellness landscape begins to change, so should we. The focus on employees and caring for their well-being has become a topic no one can escape. This is the key to increasing wholesome profitability.
- Committing to Emotional inclusion is the way forward. But tackling it in a laser-focused, sustainable way is not easy. Leaders and managers must walk the talk, and workplaces must acknowledge how much they have failed to address the Emotional wellness of employees until now.
- More leaders and organizations are taking charge as they add up the numbers and realize that the productivity impact of poor employee wellness is significant. Scaling up mental health services is now becoming the centre of focus, and value-based leadership, which takes into account the Emotional welfare of staff, is becoming the new status quo. Twitter has an in-house clinical psychologist to lead global employee wellness, Johnson & Johnson enables staff to be wellness champions looking out for each other, while Shell provides specialists that employees can go to for receiving free consultation, diagnosis, treatment, and long term management. Companies at large are becoming more emotionally connected.

- Emotional inclusion is being moulded into the new workforce normal, and its impetus lies in looking at how we can get the best of our employees and how they can perform at their best. The organizations of the future who do not do this will be left behind. Downplaying the Emotional burden is no longer an option.

- Smaller companies might sometimes think that fostering Emotional inclusion is only possible for larger organizations that have the bandwidth, but every company can promote this by opening up the discussion, inviting people to come talk about it, and directing their employees to free support platforms. Organizations, large and small, need to look into how employees' Emotional welfare is integrated into the very fabric of their workplace culture and understand that it is a direct reflection of the values they hold.

- Shifting gears from Emotional intelligence to a more action-driven, emotionally inclusive speed is where we have arrived. Momentum towards creating a proactive, emotionally inclusive workforce is gaining. The world has changed, and all of us should change with it.

Final Thoughts

'The greatest tragedy in life is not death, but a life without a purpose.'[127]

—MYLES MUNROE

My life's purpose was to bring Emotional inclusion to the world. However corny or clichéd as it may sound, it is the reason I wake up every single day. My own stories of hardship, coupled with the hundreds upon hundreds of stories I have been privy to, made it such that I could not stay quiet anymore in my efforts to humanize the workplace. And to quote inspirational speaker and author Wayne W Dyer, neither was I going to allow myself to 'die with my music still in me'[128] on the subject.

Come of this book what may, I hope that you would have seen at least some value in the need for Emotional inclusion in our organizations today. Too many of us still suffer in silence

---

[127] Munroe, Myles, as quoted by Farai Gundan in 'Dr. Myles Munroe: On Leadership, Vision, Purpose And Maximizing Your Potential', *Forbes*, (2014, November 10), https://www.forbes.com/sites/faraigundan/2014/11/10/dr-myles-munroe-on-leadership-vision-purpose-and-maximizing-your-potential/?sh=3fcb9d3180b7.

[128] Dyer, S.J., & Dyer, D.W.W. (2014) *Don't Die with Your Music Still in You: My Experience Growing Up with Spiritual Parents*, Hay House.

because showing up at work with our full selves still, illogically enough, equates to incompetency. In my own small way, I would like to change the narrative and create a humanizing revolution at work, with you onboard.

This genuine purpose feeds me with so much drive, despite it taking so much effort. Life is full, oh so full, with two children, a full-time job, and delivering Emotional inclusion to companies in a forward, laser-focused way. I am oftentimes asked how I manage it all, and my answer never fails to be the same: early mornings, lunchtimes when no business appointments are set, and evenings. To be perfectly candid with you though, it always amazes me how much energy we gain from living with purpose, from fighting for a cause we truly and deeply believe in. My greatest wish for the world is to leave behind a workplace where our Gen Z, our children, our grandchildren and future generations to come, can bring their full selves to work without having to even think about it being a modern day 'luxury'. And if we are lucky, we older folks might even get to experience it ourselves.

Let us think about it one minute. We exercise before heading into the office. We read or mediate or see friends during our lunch breaks. We pack in all of our passions and interests somewhere before bed and on the weekends. *The whole self, and nothing but the whole self.* There are noticeable symptoms of not bringing your whole self to work, did you know? We feel disconnected. We do not share our interests with others around us, even the colleagues who know us better than anyone else in the office, which means we go through the day and do not ever feel fully known. We become disengaged and unmotivated because our actions are not linked to the activities that we would do purely for the love of doing them.

We need to exercise more healthy human appreciation. To break the old, unspoken agreement between many employers and their workers to keep personal issues away from the job.

To embrace Emotional inclusion. I remain optimistic that our collective consciousness will continue to expand in a way where there will come a day where the realization is that there can be no profitable business unless this separation is demolished.

We are human beings; we are wired to feel. Disconnecting ourselves from our Emotional realms within the workplace is nothing more but a fallacy. Keeping our Emotional armours on out of fear and self-protection not only is heavy to carry but it winds up impacting our performance and the very results our companies expect from us. No one is immune to pain and human suffering. No one is immune to the ebbs and flows of human experience. You have heard me refer to 'the school of life' throughout this book; and we are all, in one way shape or form, navigating it as best we can.

What we need is an Emotional inclusion contagion. A movement of sorts where enough leaders gain the gravitas to stand up to the fact that no one is immune to the hardballs life throws at us. We learn to roll with the punches, yet I believe that we have the power within us to bring the change we wish to see in the world.

What Must Change

Gustave Le Bon once wrote that 'ideas, sentiments, emotions and beliefs possess in crowds a contagious power as intense as that of microbes'.[129] I believe this to be true and allegorically, the pandemic served as a learning for it. COVID-19 shed light on our humanity and had us all stop to take a deep introspective look into the manic and backward lives we were all pretty much living at work. We effectively had no choice but to examine our lives and rethink a more healthy and thoughtful way forward. We hear a lot

---

[129] Le Bon, G. (1968) *The Crowd: A Study of the Popular Mind*, N. S. Berg.

being spoken about reshaping the future of work. Truth be told, we were all functioning blindfolded, in what was a very archaic work model, one where we are put into conventional boxes of robotic *people of doing* instead of being *people of feeling*.

How we decide to think, feel, and believe, ultimately shapes the reality we experience. Yes, it does boil down to choices. It is thus imperative that we pick wisely, that we elect to change our collective identity, and that we redefine our 21st century organizational culture norms in a sustainable way. All the movements that have taken form stemmed from a place where enough was enough. The 'MeToo', 'Black Lives Matter', 'Stop Asian Hate' movements, and more were born from a conscious understanding that we can truly be the change we want to see in this world.

We might not have a concise roadmap as it stands today, but the decision to call out what is no longer acceptable ultimately burgeons into a conscious understanding of what must change. In our silos, we can get things done, but when we step back together to create a movement in shaping what mental health or Emotional wellness looks like both societally and in the workforce, profound paradigm shifts take place. And I know you know this, or else you would not be reading this book. Channelling our efforts in shaping a more humane workplace should be on our list of top priorities.

At the end of the day, the best way to inspire cynicism and perpetuate the ill health of our people is to fail to be emotionally inclusive. We have covered, I think widely, that it is normal to experience emotions at work—frustration, anger, fear, excitement, etc. Yet how acceptant of our emotions we are individually and how our emotions will be welcomed within our workplace ecosystems will eventually dictate the workplace of tomorrow. You might debate the fact that interpersonal fear is a very real thing—that it is normal to worry about what others think if you might need psychological help. The question however begs to be asked: who does not need psychological help at least once during their lifetime?

We human beings are so quick to judge, so quick to exclude others out of profound denial, misconception, or lack of understanding thereof. I have always thought that everyone could benefit from proper counselling, and I maintain this to this day. Someone trained, someone who is exterior to one's circle of family and friends. We are thankfully starting to witness a normalization in this arena, where people are finally starting to feel at ease talking about it. But I would not quite yet say that we are at the point yet of voicing out quite as easily that we are going to see our therapist as we would saying that we are to see our general medical practitioner for a consultation.

The Impact We Have

One of the most detrimental misconceptions surrounding mental health or Emotional wellness advocacy is the notion that advocates 'have it all together'. Although we, as Emotional wellness advocates, write and speak on some of the most vulnerable parts of ourselves, although we openly address our own struggles in the hope of spreading awareness and help others feel less alone, we are still met with judgement. We are faced with the pressure to always remain composed, to be 'self-care superstars' in our own lives.

The expectation that we must always smile even when we are sad or pretend that all is well when we are not—all these cause our mental health to plummet. This polarizing dichotomy between the perception and reality of Emotional wellness advocacy bothers me. Despite my candour regarding my experience with my own hardships, I too struggle with my mind and self-care at times. I too know the depths of pain and battle with my valleys of sorrow. It would be such a disservice and such a lie for me to say the contrary. And so unhuman of me as well.

We need to recognize that change is the only constant, it is the law of life. The success of any business will depend on the speed with which it recognizes the need to adopt change. Change that actively roots for new Emotional paradigms in the workplace. Our 'human battery' is incredibly low in this arena. The concept of Emotional inclusion is not for the psychologists alone to understand, but for all of us as business leaders as well. It is a top-down process, whether we like it or not. If we leaders cannot bravely set the note, then who will?

I dub it 'corporate leadership vulnerability'—a pledge by senior leaders to make it an integral value structure in their joint purpose to lead wholesomely, openly, and vulnerably. Regardless of whether they are introverts or extroverts, poor at sharing their emotions or great at it, leaders must make it their ethical purpose to safeguard the humanity of the people they employ by showing their humanity first. Is it scary? Yes, it is. Can it be risky? Yes. Is it worth the gamble? Well, let me put it this way: if you cannot be personal with your employees, then they will not be with you either. What is emotionally risky can also sometimes be effective in the realm of Emotional inclusion.

The outdated idea that if you experience mental health problems then you cannot hold down a job is utter nonsense. In fact, psychiatry professor Nassir Ghaemi, who has carried out extensive research on the link between mental illness and leadership, says that people suffering from a mental health illness can be great leaders[130]. Take Martin Luther King Jr, for example. The civil rights leader suffered from

---

[130] Ghaemi, N. (2011, July 30) 'Depression in Command', *The Wall Street Journal*, retrieved February 27, 2023, https://www.wsj.com/articles/SB100 01424053111904800304576474451102761640.

depression[131], but his extreme empathy—'one of the characteristics often found in people who suffer from depression'—drove him to do all he did, writes Stéphanie Thomson for the World Economic Forum[132].

The list of famous people who all struggled with mental health goes on to include a litany of greats: Virginia Woolf, Sigmund Freud, Leo Tolstoy, Edgar Allan Poe, Ernest Hemingway, to name a few. Among these luminaries, I will highlight the stories of four particularly well-known people.

- Princess Diana struggled with depression, bulimia, and self-harm due to intense scrutiny in her new role as a British royal. In a BBC interview, she admitted to feeling 'ashamed because I could not cope with the pressures'.[133]
- Abraham Lincoln was said to have battled depression most of his life, with his 'melancholy'[134] (now defined as 'depression') being a defining character trait.
- Beethoven was bipolar, and upon his increasingly apparent deafness in his mid-twenties, wrote to his brother,

---

[131] Ghaemi, N. (2012, January 16) 'Martin Luther King: Depressed and Creatively Maladjusted', *Psychology Today*, retrieved February 27, 2023, https://www.psychologytoday.com/intl/blog/mood-swings/201201/martin-luther-king-depressed-and-creatively-maladjusted.

[132] Thomson, S. (2015, October 9) '4 great leaders who had Emotional wellness problems', The World Economic Forum, retrieved February 27, 2023, https://www.weforum.org/agenda/2015/10/4-great-leaders-who-had-mental-health-problems/.

[133] Diana (1995), as quoted by Petit, S. (2021, March 30), 'Princess Diana's Panorama Interview: Biggest Bombshells', People.com, retrieved February 27, 2023, https://people.com/royals/princess-diana-bbc-panorama-interview-biggest-bombshells/.

[134] Shenk, J. W. (2005) *Lincoln's Melancholy: How Depression Challenged a President and Fueled His Greatness*, Houghton Mifflin Company.

'I joyfully hasten to meet death . . . for will it not deliver me from endless suffering?'[135]

- Van Gogh suffered from various mental illnesses, possibly including manic depression[136]. 'If I could have worked without this accursed disease, what things I might have done', the legendary artist wrote in one of his last letters.

It is not only Van Gogh and Beethoven that wrote of their pain. A more modern example is the billionaire founder of Virgin Group, Richard Branson, who is known for being publicly open about his dyslexia. In a letter contained in the book *Dear Stranger: Letters on the Subject of Happiness*, Branson—an advocate of employee wellbeing across his organization for years—writes that it is 'OK to be stressed, scared, and sad, I certainly have been throughout my life'[137]. 'I've cheated death on many adventures, seen loved ones pass away, failed in business, minced my words in front of tough audiences, and had my heart broken', he continues. 'I want to be open and honest with you, and let you know that happiness is not something just afforded to a special few. It can be yours, if you take the time to let it grow.'

Mental health problems can arise in the most enviably successful people. Again, I believe that if more people were educated around the matter, then maybe we would not be having to even talk about Emotional inclusion as it stands today. And maybe, just maybe, should we also consider that genius calls for a sprinkle of 'crazy'? I am personally completely down with that. Could we perhaps make it our purpose to embrace that too? If

---

[135] Beethoven, L. V. (1984), *Beethoven: Letters, Journals, and Conversations* (M. Hamburger, Ed.), Thames and Hudson.

[136] Wolf, P. (2001, November) 'Creativity and chronic disease Vincent van Gogh (1853–1890)', *Western Journal of Medicine*, 175(5). 10.1136/ewjm.175.5.348.

[137] *Dear Stranger: Letters on the Subject of Happiness*, 2015, Penguin.

we were to agree to this, then would it not make common sense to fully support our employees in bringing their full, imperfect selves at work?

Being flexibly accepting of each other's flawed humanity calls for us to look at Emotional inclusion through a new magnifying lens; one in which no human is taken for granted nor shamed for being different; one in which we honour and welcome our emotions as part of our birth right. This should be our north star, our collective mission in making the workplace of the future a more accepting and flourishing place to be. Let us not leave undone or forget the great power that resides in our united ability to change the archaic unspoken behaviours (often unconscious) of the workplace.

American footballer Russell Wilson writes that if we 'start being honest about our pain, our anger, and our shortcomings instead of pretending they do not exist, then maybe we'll leave the world a better place than we found it'[138]. Yes. I categorically and fundamentally believe this to be true.

We hide our negative emotions.

We ignore the sadness, pain, and anxiety.

We pretend they do not exist because of fear and shame.

But let me ask you this: what is the point of being human if you do not allow yourself to feel? Feelings and emotions do not make you weak. Being open and honest about your struggles *makes you strong*. Not weak, not unprofessional, not unfit nor unworthy. In all of us lies the power to acknowledge our distress, our fear, or even our mental health condition. I applaud all of you who have the strength to be vulnerable, real, and open about your struggles. Because it is not easy. It is brave. It is inspiring. It is the way forth toward change.

---

[138] Wilson, R. (2014, October 3) 'Let's Talk About It', *The Players' Tribune*, retrieved February 27, 2023, https://www.theplayerstribune.com/articles/lets-talk-about-it.

So, keep going. Do not let your workplace tell you how to be or feel. Embrace your mess. It makes you who you are. It is a part of your story. It has shaped you or is shaping you into the person you are becoming. And remember, sharing your story can save someone else who is silently struggling. Be the person you needed. Share the story you needed to hear. If there is something I have learned in my time on earth, it is that we are not defined by our struggles. You are not your anxiety. You are not your depression. You are not your stress. You are not your eating disorder. You are not your ADHD. You are not your medical illness. You are not your divorce. You are NOT your fill-in-the-blank. *You are an individual having a human experience.*

If you have made it to the end of this book, then allow me to invite you to now analyse your workplace and, in turn, perhaps examine where *you* could bring more Emotional inclusion to it. As acclaimed American essayist James Baldwin writes, 'Not everything that is faced can be changed, but nothing can be changed until it is faced'.[139] The injustice of our robotic workplace begs to be tackled and corrected through individual and collective action. We all play a part in taking a step, whether big or small, in becoming experts at changing our minds and acting upon materializing a brighter workplace. One that inspires employees to be who they are, fully and wholesomely. One that militates for genuine and authentic regard for the Emotional wellness of its people. Emotional inclusion is not a side topic, it is a human right. *It is your human right.* Life is just too short to be unhappy. Even at work.

---

[139] Baldwin, J. (1962, January 14) 'As much truth as one can bear', *The New York Times Book Review*, 11.

Acknowledgements

'Alone we can do so little, together we can do so much.'[140]

—Helen Keller

I could not have written this book without the support of my family, dear friends *(you know who you are)*, Dr Amy C Edmondson, whom I profoundly revere both for being the incredible woman she is and for her body of work around psychological safety, a compelling manifesto for continuous workplace humanization. I highly suggest you get your hands on her new book, *Right Kind Of Wrong: The Science of Failing Well*, and Nora Nazerene Abu Bakar, Publisher at Penguin Random House SEA. Thank you all for cheering me on during the writing process with such kindness and loving encouragement. The contents of this book benefitted immeasurably from the bold and brave stories received from Olivier Krueger, Gordon Watson, Lyn Lee, Maya Hari, Lucia Keser, Marina Matthews, Brandon Tey, Karishma Tulsidas, Yasmine Khater, Binu Balan, and Stephanie Dickson. For those of you who chose to stay anonymous, know that you are no less courageous in my eyes and that your valuable contributions will,

---

140 Keller, Helen (1981) Helen and Teacher, by Joseph P. Lash, Amer Foundation for the Blind.

without a doubt, resonate with the world and with all who aspire for a more emotionally inclusive workplace. I wish to also extend my deep gratitude to all of you who have shared your stories of hardship with me, and there have been many of you. Your stories fed and grew my belief that a workplace devoid of Emotional inclusion is a workplace devoid of humanity.

This book was no easy feat to take on—it was nothing short of a cognitive and spiritual marathon of sorts. It was one that I nevertheless took on with a great deal of responsibility, purpose, appreciation, and pride. It was a labour of love amidst the whirlwind of life I was in. Amid my divorce and dealing with the plethora of emotions that comes with it, writing on Emotional inclusion could not have come at a better time. Call it a saving grace, it allowed me to take my mind off my grief and plunge into purposeful and mission-driven writing around the meaning and need for Emotional inclusion which I have been actively advocating over the last few years, and which I so vividly lived through during the entire writing of this book. Amid this perfect storm, the love and outpouring support I received powered me on. I asked for many, many extensions, stretching my luck every single time. I particularly remember the third extension on my manuscript submission deadline. I honestly thought I would lose the book deal on the third take, but I practised what I preach, and so it went like this. It was another one of the early mornings of waking up at 2 a.m. to write, having gone to bed at 9 p.m. the night before because I do recognize the value of sleep. I made myself a coffee with absolute dread streaming through my body at the knowledge that I was not going to make my deadline on submission 'Take Two.' I was halfway through. Work engagements, showing up for my children, and going through the divorce settlements consumed my days emotionally and physically. I took my coffee outside and sat around the pool with my legs in the water, as if it would somehow wake me up faster, which it did not, and I looked up to the stars while thinking how on earth I was going to pull this one off again. I prayed. I asked for divine guidance. And I got it, what came to me was this. *Walk your talk Mollie and tell Nora what you are going through. Be honest. Stop hiding and trying to juggle it all seamlessly—because you are not. Share your Emotional burden. Whatever comes out of your honesty and selflessness will be all right.* I knew then that if I indeed did lose this book deal, I would have lost it having spoken my truth. And I made my peace with that.

While you have the book in hand today, let me share with you that it would not have been there had Nora not embraced my story with Emotional inclusion. Nor would you have it in your hands had you all not reminded me, time and time again, that we are now overdue to shed light on Emotional Inclusion. When we start practising being honest, both with our emotions and with each other, magic happens. A conspiracy of humanness forms that only those who know how to welcome Emotional inclusion will ever know.